JEFFERSON'S MANUAL OF
PARLIAMENTARY PRACTICE

FRONTISPIECE. Portrait of Thomas Jefferson, after Gilbert Stuart, George Peter Alexander Healy (1813–1894), 1860. Oil on canvas, 29.5 x 24.5 in.

Jefferson's Manual of Parliamentary Practice

by Thomas Jefferson

Edited by Brian Alexander

APPLEWOOD BOOKS

Published by Applewood Books,
an imprint of Arcadia Publishing

For a complete list of books
currently available, please visit us
at www.applewoodbooks.com

978-1-4290-3041-0

Printed in the USA

CONTENTS

Acknowledgments

Working on a project about Thomas Jefferson means engaging a community of scholars, past and present, on a subject about which nearly all of us have some knowledge and impressions. In undertaking this work on Jefferson's Manual of Parliamentary Practice, I am particularly indebted to the Robert H. Smith International Center for Jefferson Studies (ICJS) at Monticello and the guidance of ICJS's Endrina Tay, Anna Berkes, John A. Ragosta, and Whitney Pippin. J. Jefferson Looney at the Papers of Thomas Jefferson Retirement Series, James P. McClure and Bland Whitley at the Princeton Papers of Thomas Jefferson, ICJS's Andrew O'Shaughnessy, and the curators and staff at Monticello itself have provided invaluable help and insight on my numerous inquiries.

I am especially grateful to the many people at special collections and library archives across the United States and abroad who have provided their assistance—most particularly Tom Camden, Seth McCormick-Goodhart, Byron Faidley, and Lisa McCown at the Special Collections of my own institution, Washington and Lee University (W&L). I am also indebted at W&L to Madison Williams '23, a student research scholar whose efforts and talent echo throughout this project. The Lenfest Research Grant at W&L and the ICJS Jefferson Fellowship at Monticello provided essential and much-appreciated financial support toward the project. The thoughtful ideas of Alison Harvey at the University of Nevada–Reno have greatly enriched the work. Thanks to the team at Applewood Books, including publisher J. Banks Smither, for taking on the project and shepherding it through the publication process. Finally, my wife, Caroline, and our daughters, Kitty and Phoebe, have embraced Jefferson-mania at our home, making the effort more meaningful and fun.

If I have done my part to live up to the trust and support of those named above, the end result, now resting in the reader's hands, will be considered a success.

It is very material that order,
decency and regularity, be preserved
in a dignified public body.

—Jefferson's *Manual*, Section 1

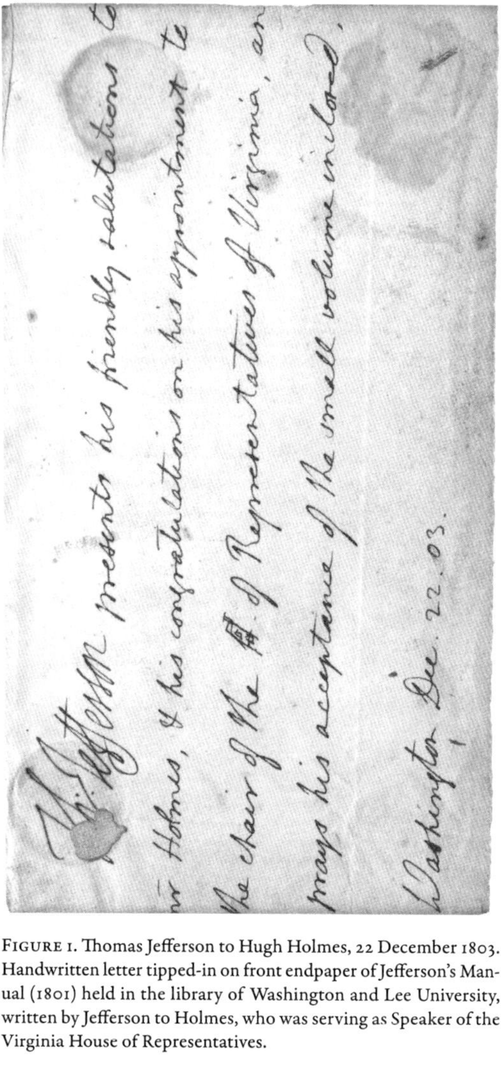

Th: Jefferson presents his friendly salutations to Mr Holmes, & his congratulations on his appointment to the chair of the H. of Representatives of Virginia, and prays his acceptance of the small volume inclosed.

Washington Dec. 22. 03.

FIGURE 1. Thomas Jefferson to Hugh Holmes, 22 December 1803. Handwritten letter tipped-in on front endpaper of Jefferson's Manual (1801) held in the library of Washington and Lee University, written by Jefferson to Holmes, who was serving as Speaker of the Virginia House of Representatives.

INTRODUCTION

JEFFERSON'S MANUAL AND THE IMPORTANCE OF RULES

BY BRIAN ALEXANDER

Thomas Jefferson's legacy in the canon of American history stems from his role in American revolutionary government, service as the third president of the United States, and, according to the inscription he authored for his gravestone, authorship of the Declaration of Independence and the Virginia Declaration of Religious Freedom, as well as the founding of the University of Virginia. Indeed, the foundations of American democracy would not be what they are if it were not for Jefferson. But democracy is only as good as its institutions. James Madison, the major author of the U.S. Constitution, knew that a government must prevent tyranny of rule by both the minority and the majority. The U.S. Congress, if it was to uphold the principles of the Constitution, could serve the American people only if it could do the same. Jefferson, who penned the infamous words of the Declaration, understood that protecting the rights of people is essential at all levels of government. This is why he wrote *A Manual of Parliamentary Practice.*

Parliamentary law is the basis for the rules of legislatures, which in the American context means first and foremost the

U.S. Congress. On this point, Thomas Jefferson made a substantial and lasting contribution to the functioning of democratic legislatures with the publication of the *Manual* in 1801. The lasting impact of Jefferson's effort comes to us in the fact that the *Manual* serves, to this day, over two hundred years later, as a precedent of the rules in both the U.S. House of Representatives and the U.S. Senate, and it has been used by legislatures across the United States and around the world since its first publication.[1] The *Manual of Parliamentary Practice* is a major, if underappreciated, aspect of Thomas Jefferson's many contributions to American democracy and the protection of rights. First published at the end of his service as vice president to John Adams, just prior to assuming his role as the third president of the United States, the manual is Jefferson's lasting testimony to the role of the U.S. Congress and to rule-based, orderly proceedings of democratic, representative legislatures.

The U.S. Constitution establishes the framework for American government—a federal union of states with a separation of powers among the legislative, executive, and judicial branches. The Constitution also provides for the Congress that "Each House may determine the Rules of its Proceedings" (Art. I Sec. 5). These parliamentary rules establish the order, determine who speaks in legislative debate, and influence which laws can be passed. By assigning each chamber to make its own

1 According to the National Conference of State Legislatures, as of 2020, Jefferson's *Manual* was used as a backup parliamentary guide for chamber procedure in at least fourteen U.S. state legislatures. Moreover, *Mason's Manual of Legislative Procedure*, currently used in seventy-nine legislative chambers, cites Jefferson's *Manual* among the parliamentary manuals and case law in its footnotes. Brenda Erickson, email to author, National Conference of State Legislatures, September 22, 2020.

rules, the Constitution leaves the House and Senate largely on their own to determine how they will operate in order to fulfill their constitutional purposes and serve the ideals of American government. The Constitution also requires that, in addition to succeeding the president in the event of removal, death, or resignation, the vice president is to serve as president of the Senate, acting as that chamber's presiding officer. In this role, the vice president may preside in the enforcement of the chamber's rules, whatever those rules may be, but they are allowed to vote only in order to break a tie.

It was in this role, seeing the necessity of order in legislative proceedings, that Jefferson wrote the *Manual* while serving as vice president to Adams, the second U.S. president, from 1797 to 1801. During the presidential administration of George Washington, Adams and Jefferson, former Revolutionary allies and friends, grew estranged over competing views on the nature of federal power. Jefferson quit service as Washington's secretary of state in 1793, opposing the emergent Federalist Party composed of Washington, his Vice President Adams, Secretary of Treasury Alexander Hamilton, and their followers, who sought a strong national government and favored a powerful president. Jefferson and allies such as James Madison favored a more republican ideal and organized into a Democratic-Republican Party, which sought to limit the power the national government held over states and opposed the "monarchist" view of presidential authority held by their Federalist adversaries. Jefferson wrote his *Manual*, in part, as a response to his concern that the strength of the executive branch should be properly checked by a rule-based legislature and his belief that a republican constitutional culture would prevail if these rules were carefully spelled out.[2]

Until the Twelfth Amendment to the Constitution was adopted in 1804, the vice presidency was filled by the person who came in second in the presidential election. This quirk meant that when Jefferson and Adams competed to succeed Washington in the presidential election of 1796, Jefferson became vice president when Adams narrowly defeated his friend-turned-rival. Jefferson then held the vice presidency until his own victory over President Adams in the closely contested election of 1800. When that election dust settled, Adams was out, Aaron Burr came in second to become vice president, and Jefferson became president.

Thomas Jefferson entered the vice presidency with a lifelong concern for republican governance, understanding the importance of rules in upholding minority rights and limiting central authority. Meanwhile, John Adams as Washington's vice president had earned a reputation for officious behavior as presiding officer of the Senate, and Jefferson feared the position was susceptible to abuse by the chair against political adversaries.[3] On taking up service in the Senate, Jefferson promised, with a brief inaugural speech on March 4, 1797, "The rules which are to govern the proceedings of this House, so far as they shall depend on me for their application, shall be applied

2 For more on the ideological intentions of Jefferson's authorship of the *Manual*, see Matthew Crow, *Thomas Jefferson, Legal History, and the Art of Recollection* (Cambridge University Press, 2017).

3 United States Senate Historical Office, "Thomas Jefferson, 2nd Vice President (1797–1801)," www.senate.gov/about/officers-staff/vice-president/VP_Thomas_Jefferson.htm.

with the most rigorous and inflexible impartiality, regarding neither persons, their views, nor principles, and seeing only the abstract proposition subject to my decision."[4] In the preface to the *Manual*, therefore, Jefferson was issuing an admonition and offering a remedy when he wrote, "The President [of the Senate] must feel weightily and seriously this confidence in his discretion; and the necessity of recurring for its government, to some known system of rules, that he may neither leave himself free to indulge caprice or passion, nor open to the imputation of them."[5]

In this spirit and from this vantage point, let us imagine Vice President Thomas Jefferson seated at the head of the Senate chamber on the second floor of Congress Hall in Philadelphia, in the final four years of the eighteenth century. The presiding officer's platform, situated at a bay in front of a central window, was beneath an extended canopy draped in crimson damask (Fig. 2). Tradition holds that Jefferson sat in an "exceptionally

---

4 Thomas Jefferson (TJ), "Address to the Senate," *Papers of Thomas Jefferson*, 4 Mar. 1797, in *The Papers of Thomas Jefferson Digital Edition*, edited by James P. McClure and J. Jefferson Looney (University of Virginia Press, Rotunda, 2008–20), rotunda-upress-virginia-edu.tjportal.idm.oclc.org/founders/TSJN.html (login required). The Papers of Thomas Jefferson are published in print and digitally in two main projects: *The Papers of Thomas Jefferson* at Princeton University (hereafter *PTJ*) or "Main Series," which comprise 1743 to the end of Jefferson's second term as president on March 4, 1809; and *The Papers of Thomas Jefferson: Retirement Series* (hereafter *PTJRS*) sponsored by the Thomas Jefferson Foundation, comprising documents from retirement from the presidency to his death in 1826. All references are to the Digital Edition. A separate topical series of the Papers of Thomas Jefferson includes works such as Jefferson's *Parliamentary Writings*, *Memorandum Books*, *Legal Commonplace*, and other works. Additional works not yet published by the *Papers* projects at the time of this research are available via the Early Access program at Founders Online, National Archives, Washington, D.C.: founders.archives.gov/about/Jefferson (hereafter Founders Online).

5 *Manual*, infra pg. 5.

FIGURE 2. Senate Chamber, Congress Hall, Philadelphia, Pennsylvania. When Philadelphia served as the temporary capital of the United States from 1790 to 1800, Congress Hall was the home of the U.S. Congress. Vice President Thomas Jefferson presided over the U.S. Senate on the dais at the front of this room until the move to the new capital in Washington, D.C., in May 1800.

tall easy chair... [with] a high, curved barrel back, no wings, and reeding on the turned arms and front legs," and upholstered in red leather. This chair is currently exhibited alongside Jefferson's artwork and other treasured items at Jefferson's home, Monticello, in Charlottesville, Virginia.[6]

From this elevated platform, Vice President Jefferson would have looked across a desk and balustrade to a place for a secretary and thirty-two individual wooden desks arranged in

6 Monticello, "Tall Easy Chair," *Thomas Jefferson Encyclopedia*, www.monticello.org/site/research-and-collections/tall-easy-chair.

two rows in a semicircle. Each desk, one for every senator of the Federalist-dominated chamber, was accompanied with an armchair upholstered in Moroccan leather joined to their wooden frames with brass nail heads exposed, a blend of function and form.[7]

The scene from his high-backed chair may have been quite to Jefferson's liking. The rectangular chamber, about forty-seven feet across by thirty-one feet deep, with walls a painted simulation of green silk, was orderly and appropriately stylish, although modest by the standards of European grandeur, elegant for the fledgling American government, and noticeably finer than the lower chamber of the House of Representatives one floor below.

From this setting, Jefferson developed what became his lasting contribution to the rules of legislatures, the *Manual of Parliamentary Practice*, a culmination of decades of his experience as a scholar and practitioner of the subject, dating back to his time as a law student in Williamsburg in the 1760s. The *Manual* builds on the well-established customs and written works of British parliamentary law, the practice of legislatures in the United States, and Jefferson's own experience to provide a system of rules for "order, decency and regularity" in legislative proceedings, complementing the limited guidelines provided by the Constitution and supplementing existing rules as they were adopted.[8]

---

7 Information on the Senate chamber is derived from Robert J. Colborn and Staff of Independence National Historical Park, *Furnishing Plan for the Second Floor of Congress Hall*, D-84 (National Park Service, October 1963). The author is indebted to Karie Diethorn, chief curator at Independence National Historical Park, in Philadelphia, for clarifying details and providing an in-person tour of Congress Hall.

8 *Manual*, infra pg. 10.

In May 1800, Philadelphia was left behind as the seat of American government for the new capital at Washington. In December of that year, in this new city, Jefferson delivered the manuscript of the *Manual* to his publisher and political ally, Samuel Harrison Smith. The *Manual* was then published on February 27, 1801, mere days before Jefferson—victorious over John Adams—became the United States' third president on March 4. Since this first publication of the book, Jefferson's influence has been a constant in parliamentary law and the rules of democratic legislatures.

A Story About Books

In March 1801, when he assumed the duties of the nation's commander-in-chief and head of the executive branch of government, Thomas Jefferson might have left behind his attention to parliamentary law. But he did not. While serving as president of the United States, Jefferson continued actively to study, promote, and refine the rules by which legislatures are governed. Evidence of this effort comes across in three copies of the 1801 edition of the *Manual* annotated in Jefferson's own hand, in his presentation of copies of that book to key political figures of the period, and in his other correspondence on the topic.[9] Looking

9 It is often said that Jefferson's only book is his *Notes on the State of Virginia* (1785). Jefferson himself contributed to this idea. Writing of the *Manual* to John W. Campbell, a Petersburg, Virginia, bookseller and printer, in 1809, he argues against including the *Manual* in Campbell's proposal to publish a complete edition of Jefferson's writings (see John W. Campbell to TJ, *PTJ*, 29 Jul. 1809). Jefferson claims, "It was a mere compilation, into which nothing entered of my own, but the arrangement, & a few observations necessary to explain that & some of the cases"

at the precise, handwritten text in the annotated copies, we can see that work Jefferson undertook while president directly led to additions made to the second edition of the *Manual*, published over a decade later in 1812. For a man who famously said, "I cannot live without books,"[10] it is appropriate that this is a story about books.

This is a story that has not been fully told until now. To date, scholars have known about and examined two copies of the 1801 edition of the *Manual* that include Jefferson's handwritten annotations—additions and corrections that he wrote into the margins of the books. One copy was kept in his private library until the end of his life, and another was presented to the Speaker of the Virginia State Senate, Francis Taliaferro Brooke, in December 1802. But a third annotated copy, previously unexamined by scholars, has now come to light in the library of Washington and Lee University. This copy was presented by Jefferson to Hugh Holmes, Speaker of the Virginia House of Delegates, in December 1803. The annotations it contains are analyzed for the first time here, in this volume.

The effort Jefferson put into researching parliamentary law and annotating his *Manual*, after its publication, was perhaps

(TJ to John W. Campbell, *PTJ*, 3 Sep. 1809). However, it is my view that, Jefferson's modesty aside, the *Manual of Parliamentary Practice* is a book by any conventional meaning of the term. The organization of the content, the original contributions by Jefferson drawn from his own research on parliamentary law, his direct experience in legislatures, and the thoroughness with which he addresses the topic, and the *Manual*'s singular, lasting impact all qualify the *Manual of Parliamentary Practice* as a book. Future scholars, museum curators, and commentators should no longer state that Jefferson authored only one book. Jefferson authored two books: *Notes on the State of Virginia* and *A Manual of Parliamentary Practice*.

10 TJ to John Adams, 10 Jun. 1815, Founders Online, founders.archives.gov/documents/Jefferson/03-08-02-0425.

not unusual for a man with interests as capacious and a mind as active as Jefferson's. For instance, in the personal copy of his *Notes on the State of Virginia*, he continued to add observations in multiple iterations long after its first publication in 1785.[11] Jefferson was a famous bibliographer of his own work, and it is because of his copious record keeping that we are fortunate to have access to many of the roughly nineteen thousand letters he wrote, not to mention farm books, account books, and other detailed records of his long life.[12] And evidence of his lengthy efforts and continued tinkering are present at that most famous Jefferson landmark, Monticello, for which he is said to have expressed great delight in "putting up, and pulling down" in decades of construction and reconstruction.[13]

More than just interesting historical artifacts, together, the three annotated copies and two authorized editions of the *Manual* help tell an important story about Jefferson's long engagement with parliamentary law and his lasting influence on the functioning of the American national legislature. In the annotated copies of the *Manual*, alongside his other correspondence, we learn about Thomas Jefferson's continued efforts, while president of the United States, as a scholar and an advocate of parliamentary law. The *Manual* reflects Jefferson's rich experience as a student and practitioner of government

---

11 Gene Zechmeister, revised by John Ragosta, "Notes on the State of Virginia," *Thomas Jefferson Encyclopedia*, www.monticello.org/site/research-and-collections/notes-state-virginia.

12 J. Jefferson Looney, "Number of Letters Jefferson Wrote," *Thomas Jefferson Encyclopedia*, 24 Mar. 2008, www.monticello.org/site/research-and-collections/number-letters-jefferson-wrote.

13 Monticello, "Architecture is my delight . . . (Quotation)," *Thomas Jefferson Encyclopedia*, www.monticello.org/site/research-and-collections/architecture-my-delightquotation.

and his appreciation of the need for a robust set of rules that a representative legislative body must have to function.

There are two editions of the *Manual* printed with Jefferson's supervision—the first published by Samuel Harrison Smith at Washington in 1801 and the second published by Joseph Milligan of Georgetown in 1812.[14] By carefully examining and dating Jefferson's annotations found in three copies of the 1801 edition and comparing the first and second editions, we can discern Jefferson's intentions regarding his final word on his *Manual*. What's more, this evidence supports a case that the second edition of 1812 should be the basis of precedent in the modern Congress and other legislatures, not the 1801 edition, as has been used. Indeed, based on the evidence developed and presented here, the edition of the *House Rules and Manual*, published for the 119th Congress in 2025, includes an update to the Jefferson's *Manual* portion that incorporates the substantive changes and new citations added by Jefferson in the 1812 version.[15]

Jefferson's Standard Goes to Print

By the time of publication of the *Manual* in 1801, Thomas Jefferson was among the most prepared people of his time to put the rules of the legislature to the page. His knowledge

14 Thomas Jefferson, *A Manual of Parliamentary Practice. For the Use of the Senate of the United States* (Samuel Harrison Smith, 1801); Thomas Jefferson, *A Manual of Parliamentary Practice. For the Use of the Senate of the United States*, 2nd ed., with the Last Additions of the Author (Joseph Milligan and William Cooper, 1812).

15 U.S. House of Representatives. *Constitution, Jefferson's Manual and Rules of the House of Representatives*, 119th Congress. Washington, DC: U.S. Government Publishing Office, 2025.

of his subject was based in early research as a law apprentice under George Wythe at Williamsburg in the 1760s, legislative service that included the House of Burgesses, the Continental Congress, the Virginia House of Delegates, the Congress of the Confederation, and, finally, president of the Senate during his tenure as John Adams's vice president.[16]

In 1797, emerging from semi-retirement at Monticello as the newly elected vice president to Adams, Jefferson assumed the role of presiding officer in the U.S. Senate. He engaged this role with characteristic commitment, immediately seeking to reestablish his familiarity with parliamentary law. Jefferson wrote to his former mentor Wythe, "It is now so long since I have acted in the legislative line that I am entirely rusty in the Parliamentary rules of procedure."[17] To update his knowledge, he sought new books on the subject and consulted his lengthy notes in his Parliamentary Pocket-Book, a personal diary of important topical ideas that he maintained across the decades of his legislative service.[18]

Jefferson assumed the vice presidency at a time when the Senate had only a limited set of rules and, consequently, in Jefferson's view the chair wielded excessive control and the majority was inadequately constrained from exercising power over the minority. As he writes in the preface to the *Manual*,

---

16 Giles Wilkeson Gray, "Thomas Jefferson's Interest in Parliamentary Practice," *Speech Monographs* 27, no. 5 (1960), 318–19; Wilbur Samuel Howell, ed., *Jefferson's Parliamentary Writings: "Parliamentary Pocket-Book" and a Manual of Parliamentary Practice*, Papers of Thomas Jefferson, Second Series (Princeton University Press, 1988), 3–4; Thomas Jefferson, "Report on Parliamentary Procedure," *PTJ*, 8 Nov.–8 Dec. 1769.

17 TJ to George Wythe, *PTJ*, 22 Jan. 1797.

18 Howell, *Parliamentary Writings*, 10.

"This places under the discretion of the President [of the Senate] a very extensive field of decision, and one which, irregularly exercised, would have a powerful effect on the proceedings and determinations of the House."[19] With "wisely" constructed rules, the presiding officer, as noted, "may neither leave himself free to indulge caprice or passion, nor open to the imputation of them."[20] Jefferson reemphasizes this theme, in Section 1, as a key precept of the *Manual*: "the only weapons by which the minority can defend themselves against similar attempts from those in power, are the forms and rules of proceeding... by a strict adherence to which, the weaker party can only be protected from those irregularities and abuses."[21] Whether Jefferson had in mind John Adams, Federalist rival and predecessor as the Senate's presiding officer, or his future successors, a legislature open to abuse by the chair or the majority is one vulnerable to despotism. In a representative legislature, a system of rules not only improves order in proceedings but also restrains the power of individual leaders and protects the minority and thereby serves the broader ideals of republican governance.

By early 1800, Jefferson had determined to put his accumulated wisdom into a manual that, as he wrote to Wythe, "I mean to deposit with the Senate as the Standard by which I judge, and am willing to be judged."[22] Throughout 1800, Jefferson worked "long and systematically" to complete the *Manual* by the end of his Senate service. In writing the book, Jefferson drew from his Parliamentary Pocket-Book; readings in at least sixty sources

19 *Manual*, infra pg. 5.
20 Ibid.
21 *Manual*, infra pg. 10.
22 TJ to George Wythe, *PTJ*, 28 Feb. 1800.

in law and parliamentary procedure; further consultation with figures such as Wythe, Edmund Pendleton, and House Clerk John Beckley; and, of course, his active service as the presiding officer in the Senate.[23]

In December 1800, he delivered his manuscript to Smith for publication. Jefferson was received in the parlor of the Smith home on Capitol Hill by the publisher's wife, Margaret Bayard Smith, of the prominent Bayard family. A noteworthy woman of letters herself, Bayard Smith writes that Jefferson's "original was in his own neat, plain, but elegant hand writing."[24] Decades later, Bayard Smith noted that the manuscript "is still preserved by Mr. Smith and valued as a precious relique." If this handwritten manuscript has survived, its present whereabouts are unknown; perhaps an important discovery awaits future scholars.

We can estimate that Smith printed 100 copies of the *Manual*. Writing to Smith on December 21, 1800, Jefferson said, "He will ask of mr Smith either to print him 100. copies at his own

23 TJ to Edmund Pendleton, *PTJ*, 19 Apr. 1800; John Beckley to TJ, *PTJ*, 15 Mar. 1798; Dumas Malone, *Jefferson and the Ordeal of Liberty* (Little, Brown and Company, 1962), 454. Jefferson's collection of parliamentary writings was substantial: "Respect for Jefferson increases when a check of the catalogue of the Library of Congress in 1815, consisting of books recently purchased from him by the Government, discloses the fact that he had personally owned most of the books listed among his citations [in the *Manual*]" (Everett S. Brown, "Jefferson's *Manual of Parliamentary Practice*," *Michigan Alumnus: Quarterly Review* 49, no. 15 [1943]: 147.) For reasons such as this, Wilbur Samuel Howell rightly claims that "TJ must also be considered the foremost American scholar of his time in the field of parliamentary law" (Howell, *Parliamentary Writings*, 348). The number of sixty works used by Jefferson in writing the *Manual* is based on the present author's cross-referencing of Jefferson's abbreviations within the text of the book against a list of Jefferson's parliamentary sources in Howell, *Parliamentary Writings*, xv–xxvii.

24 Margaret Bayard Smith, *The First Forty Years of Washington Society, Portrayed by the Family Letters of Mrs. Samuel Harrison Smith*, edited by Gaillard Hunt (Charles Scribner's Sons, 1906), 8.

expence, or for mr Smith to print it on his own account & let Th: J. have 75. copies at the selling price."[25] Nearer to the book's release, on February 23, 1801, Jefferson wrote to Smith, "The bookbinder promises me 40. copies of the Manual on Thursday morning. your's therefore might be offered for sale on Saturday."[26] Though the record is not precisely clear, it appears most likely that Smith printed the higher quantity of 100, with Jefferson acquiring 40 for himself. Years later, in 1811, Jefferson had at least 24 copies in his possession, which he provided to the Richmond bookseller William Prichard.[27] The story of the path that many of these 100 copies took, told below, tells us something of the demand for Jefferson's work, as well as his own efforts to promote it.

The President as Scholar of Parliamentary Law

The publication of the *Manual* at the end of Jefferson's vice presidency could have been the culmination and final word of Jefferson's long work as a scholar and practitioner of parliamentary law. However, as evidence newly presented here suggests, in the early years of his presidency, Jefferson continued to research and promote the orderly manner by which legislatures ought to conduct themselves. With the three annotated copies of the *Manual* and close examination of the historical record, including evidence about the people to whom Jefferson presented copies of

25 TJ to Samuel Harrison Smith, *PTJ*, 21 Dec. 1800.
26 TJ to Samuel Harrison Smith, *PTJ*, 23 Feb. 1801.
27 TJ to William Prichard, *PTJRS*, 8 Jul. 1812.

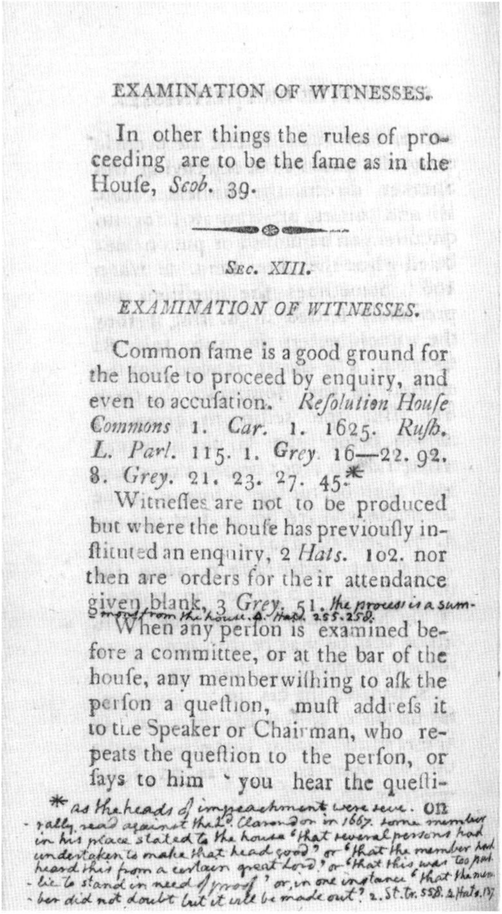

EXAMINATION OF WITNESSES.

In other things the rules of proceeding are to be the same as in the House, *Scob.* 39.

SEC. XIII.

EXAMINATION OF WITNESSES.

Common fame is a good ground for the house to proceed by enquiry, and even to accusation. *Resolution House Commons* 1. *Car.* 1. 1625. *Rush. L. Parl.* 115. 1. *Grey.* 16—22. 92. 8. *Grey.* 21. 23. 27. 45.*

Witnesses are not to be produced but where the house has previously instituted an enquiry, 2 *Hats.* 102. nor then are orders for their attendance given blank, 3 *Grey.* 51. the process is a summons from the house. 4. Hats. 255.258.

When any person is examined before a committee, or at the bar of the house, any member wishing to ask the person a question, must address it to the Speaker or Chairman, who repeats the question to the person, or says to him 'you hear the questi-on

* as the heads of impeachment were severally read against the Ld. Clarendon in 1667. some member in his place stated to the house 'that several persons had undertaken to make that head good' or 'that the member had heard this from a certain great Lord' or 'that this was too publick to stand in need of proof' or, in one instance 'that the member did not doubt but it will be made out.' 2. St. Tr. 558. 4 Hats. 137

FIGURE 3. Jefferson's *Manual* (1801) (detail, Section 13), with annotations to the text by Thomas Jefferson, Library of Congress.

the book, we can say that Jefferson was, in fact, quite focused and deliberate in his work on the topic during the first years of his presidency. In particular, having recently acquired and read the fourth volume of John Hatsell's *Precedents of Proceedings in the House of Commons* (London, 1796), Jefferson updated his previous research based on new information.[28]

We see President Jefferson's efforts as a scholar of parliamentary law, literally, in books. Individual copies of the 1801 *Manual* provide physical evidence of Jefferson's scholarship and promotion of his subject well into the years of his presidency. The physical copies of each annotated book, including the dates on which two were presented to legislative leaders from Virginia, convey a story of the timing and nature of President Jefferson's research and efforts. The extent of the annotations in each copy corresponds with the length of time the copy was in Jefferson's

---

28 A letter from Jefferson to publisher Matthew Carey on January 27, 1812, created some subsequent confusion for later Jefferson scholars. In it, Jefferson wrote, "I had never seen Hatsell's 3d volume" (TJ to Mathew Carey, *PTJRS*, 27 Jan. 1812), when he plainly meant the fourth volume published in 1796. In fact, Hatsell's third volume is referenced throughout the 1801 edition of the *Manual*. Contributing to the confusion, a letter from TJ to Milligan (*PTJRS*, 7 Jan. 1812), in which he stated that he "had never yet seen the 4th vol. of Hatsell," was not available at the time Sowerby catalogued Jefferson's books in the 1950s, and both the 1815 Jonathan Elliot and the Nicholas P. Trist catalogues of the library also list only Hatsell's three-volumes-in-one, not the fourth. See Howell, *Parliamentary Writings*, 32 Fn. 99; Emily Millicent Sowerby, *Catalogue of the Library of Thomas Jefferson*, 3 vols. (Library of Congress, 1952); Thomas Jefferson and Nicholas Philip Trist, *Catalogue* (1823), manuscript/mixed material (Library of Congress), www.loc.gov/item/87204942; see Entry 384, at page 80 of 139. This has resulted in scholars such as Sowerby (183, Entry 2894) and Malone (456 Fn. 49) overlooking the fourth volume in Jefferson's collections and scholarly work. Subsequently, the Library has catalogued Hatsell vol. 4 with the Jefferson Exhibit under Sowerby 2894 (Library of Congress, Catalog, lccn.loc.gov/2014660852). See: John Hatsell, *Precedents of Proceedings in the House of Commons; Under Separate Titles; with Observations*, vol. 4, Relating to Conference, and Impeachment (T. Payne, T. Cadell, Jun., and W. Davies, 1796).

possession and supports the argument that Jefferson continued to add notes and corrections as his reading on the topic progressed. In other words, it was an ongoing effort, not just a one-time activity. Careful examination of these copies provides a window into the mind and intentions of the third president.

THE LIBRARY OF CONGRESS COPY.

The first of the annotated copies, currently in the collection at the Library of Congress, contains thirty-eight annotations handwritten by Jefferson, the most of the three (Fig. 3). The Library copy of the annotated *Manual* is arguably Jefferson's true personal copy. Based on analysis of markings in the book and the date the Library of Congress acquired it, it is likely to have been in Jefferson's possession at Monticello until the end of his life in 1826.[29] It is the only among the three annotated copies containing Jefferson's private bookmark (figs. 4a and 4b). In this "secret" mark of ownership, Jefferson wrote his initials, "T" and "J," adjacent to the "I" and "T" printer's marks that helped with the assembly of the gatherings of pages into a bound book.[30] It is listed as Copy 4 in the catalogue of the Thomas Jefferson Papers at the Library of Congress. Jefferson retained this personal copy and held it back from the sale of his books to the Library of Congress in 1815. It is part of the "Retirement Library" or "Supplemental Library" acquired by the Library of Congress after Jefferson's death.

29 Howell, when discussing the Jefferson annotation at section 52, refers to the Brooke copy as "his own personal copy" (Howell, *Parliamentary Writings*, 432). However, while the Brooke copy was among the copies possessed by TJ, it had been given away by December 1802.

30 Douglas L. Wilson, *Jefferson's Books* (Thomas Jefferson Foundation, 1996), 47.

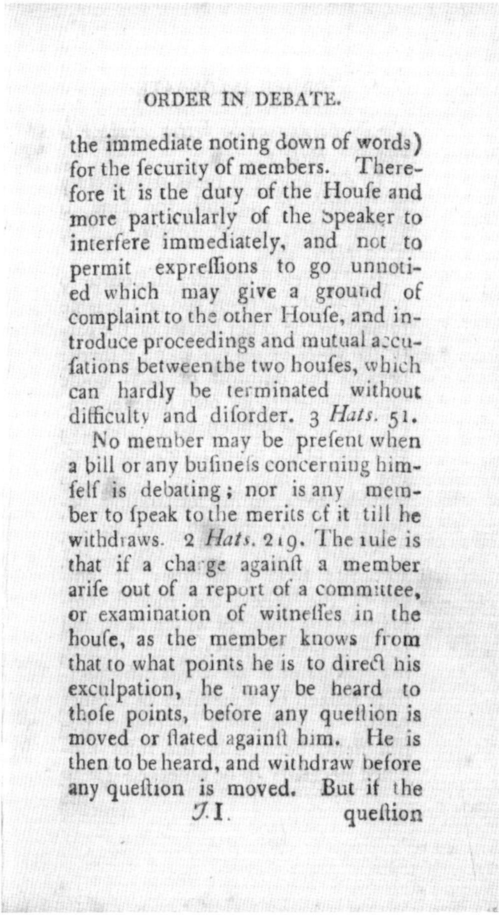

ORDER IN DEBATE.

the immediate noting down of words) for the ſecurity of members. Therefore it is the duty of the Houſe and more particularly of the Speaker to interfere immediately, and not to permit expreſſions to go unnotied which may give a ground of complaint to the other Houſe, and introduce proceedings and mutual accuſations between the two houſes, which can hardly be terminated without difficulty and diſorder. 3 *Hats.* 51.

No member may be preſent when a bill or any buſineſs concerning himſelf is debating; nor is any member to ſpeak to the merits of it till he withdraws. 2 *Hats.* 219. The rule is that if a charge againſt a member ariſe out of a report of a committee, or examination of witneſſes in the houſe, as the member knows from that to what points he is to direct his exculpation, he may be heard to thoſe points, before any queſtion is moved or ſtated againſt him. He is then to be heard, and withdraw before any queſtion is moved. But if the

J.I. queſtion

FIGURE 4A. Jefferson's private bookmarks in his personal copy of the *Manual* (detail, Section 17), Library of Congress, in Washington, D.C.

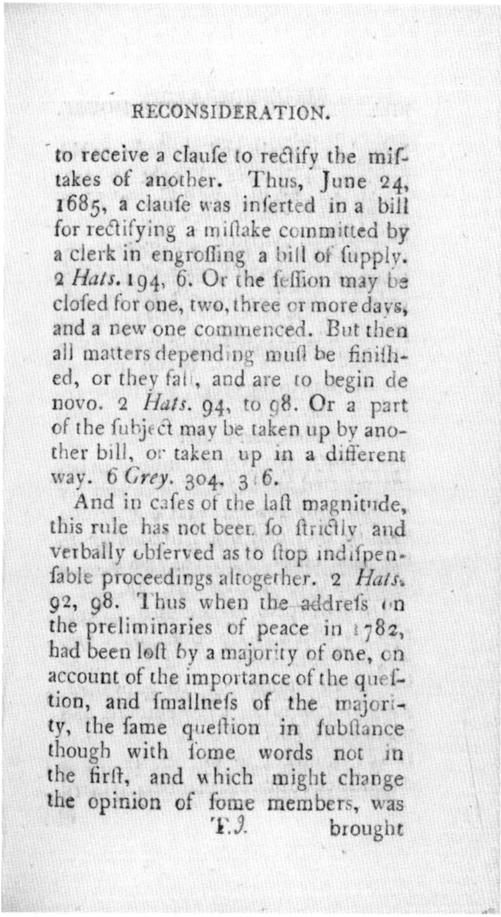

RECONSIDERATION.

to receive a clauſe to rectify the miſtakes of another. Thus, June 24, 1685, a clauſe was inſerted in a bill for rectifying a miſtake committed by a clerk in engroſſing a bill of ſupply. 2 *Hats.* 194, 6. Or the ſeſſion may be cloſed for one, two, three or more days, and a new one commenced. But then all matters depending muſt be finiſhed, or they fall, and are to begin de novo. 2 *Hats.* 94, to 98. Or a part of the ſubject may be taken up by another bill, or taken up in a different way. 6 *Grey.* 304, 316.

And in caſes of the laſt magnitude, this rule has not been ſo ſtrictly and verbally obſerved as to ſtop indiſpenſable proceedings altogether. 2 *Hats.* 92, 98. Thus when the addreſs on the preliminaries of peace in 1782, had been loſt by a majority of one, on account of the importance of the queſtion, and ſmallneſs of the majority, the ſame queſtion in ſubſtance though with ſome words not in the firſt, and which might change the opinion of ſome members, was

T.J. brought

FIGURE 4B. Jefferson's private bookmarks in his personal copy of the *Manual* (detail, Section 43), Library of Congress, in Washington, D.C.

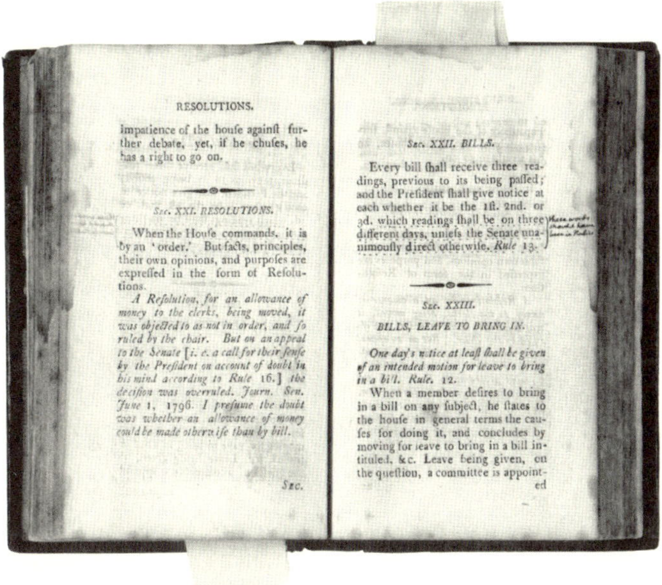
RESOLUTIONS.

impatience of the houſe againſt further debate, yet, if he chuſes, he has a right to go on.

Sec. XXI. RESOLUTIONS.

When the Houſe commands, it is by an 'order.' But facts, principles, their own opinions, and purpoſes are expreſſed in the form of Reſolutions.

A Reſolution, for an allowance of money to the clerks, being moved, it was objected to as not in order, and ſo ruled by the chair. But on an appeal to the Senate [i. e. a call for their ſenſe by the Preſident on account of doubt in his mind according to Rule 16.] the deciſion was overruled. Journ. Sen. June 1, 1796. I preſume the doubt was whether an allowance of money could be made otherwiſe than by bill.

Sec.

Sec. XXII. BILLS.

Every bill ſhall receive three readings, previous to its being paſſed; and the Preſident ſhall give notice at each whether it be the 1ſt. 2nd. or 3d. which readings ſhall be on three different days, unleſs the Senate unanimouſly direct otherwiſe. *Rule* 13.

Sec. XXIII.

BILLS, LEAVE TO BRING IN.

One day's notice at leaſt ſhall be given of an intended motion for leave to bring in a bill. Rule. 12.

When a member deſires to bring in a bill on any ſubject, he ſtates to the houſe in general terms the cauſes for doing it, and concludes by moving for leave to bring in a bill intituled, &c. Leave being given, on the queſtion, a committee is appointed

FIGURE 5. Jefferson's *Manual* (1801) (detail, Section 22), with annotations to the text by Jefferson, presented to Francis Taliaferro Brooke, 20 December 1802.

THE BROOKE COPY.

A second copy of the *Manual* with Jefferson's annotations is in private collection but was originally presented by Jefferson to Francis Taliaferro Brooke, Speaker of the Virginia Senate, on December 20, 1802.[31] This Brooke copy has the fewest annotations among the three, in two sections on two leaves, and was

31 TJ to Francis Taliaferro Brooke, *PTJ*, 20 Dec. 1802. The Brooke copy was last known for public sale by Bauman Rare Books in Las Vegas in 2012 at a retail price of $268,000 (Laura Carroll, "Bauman Rare Books Pays Homage to Past U.S. Presidents," *Las Vegas Review-Journal*, 19 Oct. 2012, www.reviewjournal.com/business/bauman-rare-books-pays-homage-to-past-u-s-presidents).

in Jefferson's possession the shortest duration. It serves as the first indicator that Jefferson likely pursued his research and made his notes over a period of time. (Fig. 5)

The Holmes Copy.

The third and last known copy of the *Manual* annotated by Jefferson is the one analyzed here for the first time. This copy was presented by Jefferson to Hugh Holmes, Speaker of the Virginia House of Representatives, on December 22, 1803.[32] This Holmes copy has ten annotations, substantially more than the Brooke but fewer than the Library copy (Fig. 6). This copy also contains Jefferson's original letter of presentation to Holmes adhered to the front pastedown endpaper (Fig. 1).[33] The Holmes copy was in private collection until it was donated to Washington and Lee University by James J. White III, an alumnus of the class of 1951. Wilbur Samuel Howell did not include this copy in his exhaustive study of Jefferson's parliamentary writings, and until now, the content of the annotations has not been analyzed or publicly available.

32 TJ to Hugh Holmes, *Papers PTJ*, 22 Dec. 1803.

33 In Jefferson's handwritten letter, the apparent figure of a house is drawn in the capital "H" of "House of Representatives." It is unclear whether Jefferson himself or a later owner would have inserted this playful doodle. Credit goes to Endrina Tay at ICJS for first pointing out this curious marking.

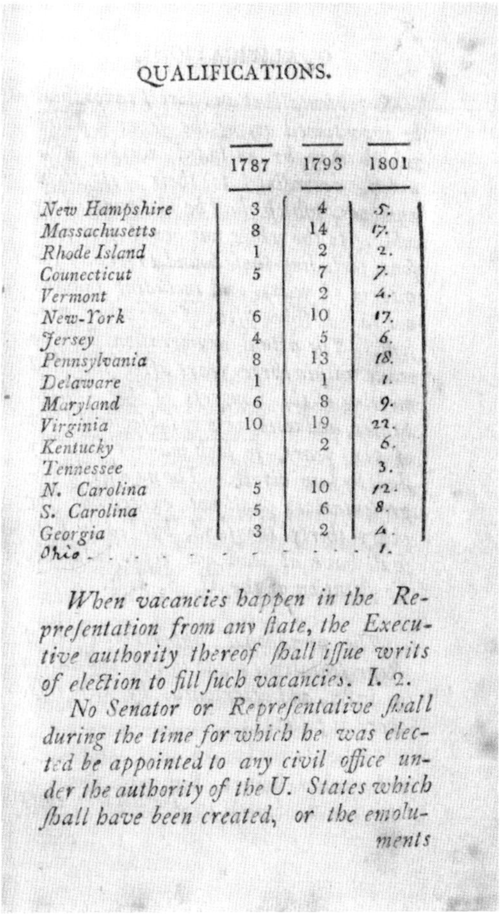

QUALIFICATIONS.

	1787	1793	1801
New Hampshire	3	4	5.
Massachusetts	8	14	17.
Rhode Island	1	2	2.
Counecticut	5	7	7.
Vermont		2	4.
New-York	6	10	17.
Jersey	4	5	6.
Pennsylvania	8	13	18.
Delaware	1	1	1.
Maryland	6	8	9.
Virginia	10	19	22.
Kentucky		2	6.
Tennessee			3.
N. Carolina	5	10	12.
S. Carolina	5	6	8.
Georgia	3	2	4.
Ohio			1.

When vacancies happen in the Repreſentation from any ſtate, the Executive authority thereof ſhall iſſue writs of election to fill ſuch vacancies. I. 2.

No Senator or Repreſentative ſhall during the time for which he was elected be appointed to any civil office under the authority of the U. States which ſhall have been created, or the emolu-

ments

FIGURE 6. Jefferson's *Manual* (1801) (detail, Section 5), presented to Hugh Holmes, 22 December 1803. Jefferson wrote the number of representatives in the column for 1801. The book was published before the apportionment, so the column was printed blank.

"Where They Agree and Where They Vary":[34] *Understanding the Annotations*

In total, the annotations indicate a story of Jefferson the President continuing to read and reflect on his *Manual* and his efforts to promote parliamentary law in his home state of Virginia and beyond. The level of detail Jefferson put into marking up these three volumes suggests the focus and purpose that he brought to this significant effort. Collectively, the annotations reflect not a passing interest but the technical and ideological concern the third president of the United States placed on the rules and procedures of the legislative branch of government.

We learn from these physical copies of the book that Jefferson's annotations grew cumulatively, expanding from notes on only a couple of leaves in the Brooke copy (1802) to the additional notes on multiple pages of the Holmes copy (1803) to the further annotations in the personal copy (1826) now at the Library of Congress. Together, Jefferson's annotations suggest that he continued to read on parliamentary law at least through December 1803, when he presented the Holmes copy, as well as beyond, up to some uncertain date of the additional notes in the Library copy.

The precise dates of Jefferson's annotations to each copy are not known. Letters of presentation to Brooke and Holmes are each marked "Washington," and Jefferson's travel itinerary indicates that he was in Washington, D.C., in December of both 1802 and 1803.[35] This strongly suggests that he wrote

34 *Manual*, infra pg. 6.

35 James A. Bear Jr. and Lucia C. Stanton, eds., *Jefferson's Memorandum Books: Accounts, with Legal Records and Miscellany, 1767–1826* (Princeton University Press, 1997), 1:lii.

the letters and sent the annotated copies from the President's House, as the White House was commonly known at that time. It is rather remarkable, then, to consider that President Jefferson, at the same time he was engaged in historical events such as negotiating the Louisiana Purchase and commissioning the Lewis and Clark expedition, was also making additions to his book on parliamentary law and distributing copies of it to other political notables of the age.

Importantly, close analysis reveals that the texts of the handwritten annotations appear almost in their entirety in the new text added to the second edition of the *Manual* published in 1812.[36] This means that the work Jefferson did while president, beginning almost as soon as the first edition was published and culminating several years thereafter, helped him revise the work for its second edition a decade later.[37]

If he maintained a separate handwritten copy of the annotations, beyond what was in the Library copy, there is no evidence of this in the existing known record. However, Jefferson did have a separate list of the additions printed in February 1806. An invoice from Samuel Harrison Smith to Jefferson, dated February 18, includes a line item dated "Feb. To printing additions to Manual—[lre?] Quarter sheet foolscap—500

36 Although he continued to compile his Parliamentary Pocket-Book into the early 1800s (Howell, *Parliamentary Writings*, 43; see also 334, note to Para. 583–84), new text of the annotations does not appear in the Pocket-Book aside from six entries drawn from Hatsell, vol. 4, evidently written after 1801 (160–61, paras. 583–88).

37 The 1801 edition was reprinted during the interim by others (e.g. see Howell, *Parliamentary Writings*, 434–35), but only the 1812 Milligan printing can be called the true second edition, done with Jefferson's authorization and input and inclusive of his additions.

Copies."[38] In an exchange with John Minor, a member of the Virginia House of Delegates, Minor requests a copy of Jefferson's *Manual* on February 5, 1806.[39] In his reply to Minor, honoring the request, on March 2, 1806, Jefferson writes, "I have delayed sending you a copy of the Manual until I could get printed a couple of supplementary leaves which are inserted in the copy I now inclose you."[40]

Jefferson references the printed supplement again four years later. In 1810, he provides an enclosure of "a little supplement for every copy of two leaves" in delivering copies of the Smith edition to William Prichard, the Richmond bookseller.[41] Jefferson again alludes to a printed copy of "useful additions" that he provided the publisher Joseph Milligan for preparation of the 1812 edition and then again in a letter to Mathew Carey that same January.[42] A copy of the supplementary leaves is not currently known to exist, and no other surviving list of Jefferson's additions and corrections is currently known outside what can be discerned in the three annotated copies and, later, in additions to the 1812 second edition. It would be a fine discovery, indeed, if a handwritten or printed copy of Jefferson's additions were to be found.

In total, thirty-eight annotations were written by Jefferson and twenty-two appeared in print in the 1812 second edition.

38 Samuel Harrison Smith to TJ, Founders Online, 18 Feb. 1806; the author thanks Bland Whitley and Martha King at Princeton for bringing this record to his attention.

39 John Minor to TJ, *PTJ*, 5 Feb. 1806.

40 TJ to John Minor, *PTJ*, 2 Mar. 1806.

41 TJ to William Prichard, *PTJRS*, 6 Dec. 1810.

42 TJ to Joseph Milligan, *PTJRS*, 7 Jan. 1812; TJ to Mathew Carey, *PTJRS*, 27 Jan. 1812.

There are fifteen handwritten annotations, consisting of references to vol. 4 of Hatsell's *Precedents,* which Jefferson made to his personal (Library) copy of the 1801 *Manual* that do not appear in the 1812 second edition, for reasons unknown. Another single annotation made by Jefferson, on the Treaty of Pardo at section 52, appears in the Brooke copy of the 1801 edition and was not included in the Milligan 1812 edition. Editor's notes in the present edition of the *Manual* indicate all additional text, where it appears as annotations in the three copies of the 1801 first edition of the *Manual,* and whether it appears in Milligan's 1812 second edition either verbatim or with variation, or if it is absent.

The annotations to copies of the *Manual* illustrate Jefferson's continued scholarship on parliamentary law, beginning in the early days of his presidency. Jefferson's annotations are all carefully entered such that they can be easily read as part of the existing printed typeface. It is readily evident, especially as the detail repeats across the copies, that these were not incidental marginalia or reading notes but additions that Jefferson intended to be included with the original text. They range from clearly articulated new phrases, sentences, or paragraphs to multiple new references to vol. 4 of Hatsell's *Precedents.*[43] The evidence

43 As late as September 1800, still two months before delivering his manuscript to Smith, Jefferson may not have had Hatsell's fourth volume in his possession, as suggested when he referenced only three volumes of Hatsell in a list of readings he compiled for Joseph C. Cabell ("A Course of Reading for Joseph C. Cabell," *PTJ,* Sep. 1800). When he acquired a copy is uncertain, but he likely began reading it sometime after publication but prior to the presentation to Holmes. Jefferson continued to provide updates to Smith for publication into February 1801, evidenced by references in Section 52 to events in the Senate on January 6 and February 3 of that year (see *Manual,* 1801, Para. 52.10 and 52.11; TJ to Samuel Harrison Smith, *PTJ,* 6 Jan. 1801). Given the late date of these updates to Smith, the absence of

of the annotations indicates that Jefferson's work was ongoing over an extended period. The Library copy, with its thirty-eight annotations, supports a compelling case that Jefferson continued to read and reflect on parliamentary law beyond the point at which he presented the Holmes copy in December 1803. The reader is referred to the "Editorial Method" in this volume for detailed analysis of Jefferson's annotations across the three copies.

We learn from the annotations and new content of the 1812 second edition of the *Manual* several aspects of Jefferson's continued thinking on parliamentary law, in particular what he drew from his new reading of Hatsell vol. 4. Together, these additions illustrate Jefferson's focus on the importance of rules, concerns for the protection of minorities, and attention to the technical qualities of parliamentary procedure. For instance, in the 1801 edition, Jefferson emphasizes his concern for the importance of rules "not subject to the caprice of the Speaker, or captiousness of the members."[44] In a new passage in section 1, handwritten in the Holmes and Library copies and published in the 1812 second edition, Jefferson states that "[m]atters of form are essential to government" and that rules and customs, whatever they may be, are important in providing uniformity to parliamentary proceedings. Other additions to 1812 based on his annotations provide new references to precedent and appear in sections, for example, on the examination of witnesses, consideration of bills, and amendments. In section 26, "Bills, Commitment," Jefferson offers a new statement on allowing members to hear witnesses

---

any reference to vol. 4 of Hatsell in them suggests he still had not researched the volume.

44 *Manual*, infra pg. 10.

before select committees, writing, "though any members may be present at the examination of witnesses, they may not be at the debate, disposition or penning of the business by the select committee."[45] Several new additions to the 1812 edition based on his annotations pertain to conference committees, drawing from a major topic of Hatsell vol. 4, and indicating Jefferson's attention to the process of resolving bills in a bicameral legislature before they can be sent to the executive branch for signature into law or veto. While perhaps seeming minor, this detailed attention to parliamentary procedure is actually significant in light of Jefferson's belief that rules are a protection against the abuse of power. The close attention Jefferson paid to matters such as decorum and order would facilitate the attainment of loftier republican ideals and the protection of minority and majority rights in a representative legislature.

We also know that Jefferson consulted volumes on parliamentary law at least as late as 1805. In the second term of his presidency, he was prompted to do so by Hugh Holmes, the recipient of the second annotated copy. Holmes, still serving in the Virginia House of Delegates, proved a diligent student of the *Manual*, writing to Jefferson on November 18, 1805, to settle a question on the meaning of a passage in section 17, "Order in Debate." Holmes writes:

> The Manual, which you did Me the honor to present on My election to the Chair of the house of Delegates of Virginia in 1803 so remarkable for its perspicuity when the author of the compilation himself speaks contains a quotation

45 *Manual*, infra pg. 52.

> from Hats. 169. 170 (to be found in your Manual section 17) which in some degree perplexed Me on a sudden call for a decision on its subject, either because at that Moment from the delicacy of the occurrence My Mind did not bear directly on the subject and Might really have been obscured on the clause quoted was itself doubtfull from the language employed—Here is the clause—"No person is to use indecent Language, against the proceedings of the house, No prior determination of which, is to be reflected On by Any Member, unless he Means to conclude with a Motion to rescind it." I supposed that reflections on an *Act* of the preceding Legislature, No Motion being then before the house to rescind the same, were Not in Order and that such *prior determination*, was Meant to be secured against reflection, because a case of rescinding a determination of the existing house could Not happen inasmuch as Another rule "that No decision of the house can Again be drawn in question during the same session" forbids such rescinding. But I fear I have Mistaken the construction and will be very thankfull to be set right by your Opinion on these questions.[46]

Jefferson was unprepared to respond to such a detailed inquiry, replying, "I am too rusty in Parliamentary learning to have much confidence in my opinions on subjects of that kind."[47] Yet he was determined to assist the member of the Virginia legislature, adding, "To satisfy myself more fully I went to the Capitol &

46 Hugh Holmes to TJ, *PTJ*, 18 Nov. 1805, advance copy, not finalized; provided with courtesy by Bland Whitley to the author, 11 Jun. 2020.

47 TJ to Hugh Holmes, *PTJ*, 3 Dec. 1805.

consulted Hatsel [*sic*] from whom the Manual quotes it; and there, the text as well as a note being more extensive & particular, all doubt was removed; the rule being evidently restrained to indecent language against the proceedings of *the same house*, and not extending to those of a former one."[48]

Whether any of his findings on this trip led to new material for the additions he made to the *Manual* cannot be determined from available evidence. What is remarkable, however, is that the sitting president of the United States, in the first year of his second term, made the two-mile trek to Capitol Hill to consult available books on parliamentary law in response to a query from an interested state legislator about order in parliamentary debate. This not only suggests something about the character of Thomas Jefferson, but it also seems an act hard to imagine any modern president undertaking.[49]

---

48 TJ to Hugh Holmes, *PTJ*, 3 Dec. 1805.

49 The episode also provides a clue to as to the books Jefferson kept at the President's House. That he had to travel to the Capitol to consult Hatsell indicates that his personal copy was probably at Monticello.

The President's Promotion of Parliamentary Law

Jefferson was not only a scholar and a practitioner of parliamentary law, but he was also active in promoting it. Evidence of Jefferson's effort to promote parliamentary law beyond the "deposit" of his *Manual* at the Senate is represented in his correspondence and distribution of copies of the book. Physical manifestation of this interest in the promotion of order and decorum in debate is evident in the presentation of the two annotated copies of the *Manual* to the leaders of the Virginia state legislature. Although he modestly puts them forward to Speaker Brooke and Leader Holmes, writing to the latter that "the little volume ... may be a convenience,"[50] it is evident that he sought to extend his example of a good system of parliamentary rules to the legislature of his home state by the choice and the audience of his gift.

Other evidence of Jefferson's promotion of parliamentary law lies in additional cases where President Jefferson presented gifts of his *Manual* in the United States and abroad. In collections of Jefferson's papers, we see presentations and references to gifts of the *Manual* to several leading figures of the day. For instance, Brooke, Holmes, and John Minor, already mentioned, were not the only recipients in the Virginia statehouse to whom Jefferson provided his *Manual*. Writing from Washington on October 25, 1801, Jefferson presented a copy to his nephew Peter Carr, then a representative in the Virginia House of Delegates from Albemarle County. Jefferson included a second copy for Peter Johnston, also a representative in the Virginia House, who would later succeed Hugh Holmes as its Speaker from 1805

50 TJ to Francis Taliaferro Brooke, *PTJ*, 20 Dec. 1802.

to 1807.[51] Jefferson presented a copy to yet another statesman from Virginia, Edmund Harrison, probably sometime in late 1802. In a letter of thanks from Richmond, dated December 30, 1802, Harrison "presents his respectful acknowledgments to Mr. Jefferson,—thanks him for the parliamentary Manual, which is enhanced in value from the polite and friendly manner in which it was presented."[52] Harrison was a representative in the Virginia House of Delegates, originally from Prince George County, but then serving for Amelia County; he served as Speaker in 1802–03, at the time when he received the *Manual* from Jefferson.[53]

An extensive search of library archives and auction records reveals additional instances of President Jefferson's distribution of the first edition of his *Manual* to members of legislative bodies and key figures of government. In the spring of 2021, seventy existing copies of the 1801 edition of the *Manual* were identified, among which there were at least twenty presentation copies.[54] The Holmes and Brooke copies stand uniquely as the only known annotated presentation copies. Other presentation examples, dating to 1803, include a copy Jefferson gave to Dwight Foster, a Massachusetts Federalist who served in the U.S. Senate; a copy given by Jefferson to James Hillhouse, a prominent Connecticut Federalist politician and member of Congress; and a copy presented to Theodore Foster, one of

---

51 TJ to Peter Carr, *PTJ*, 25 Oct. 1801.

52 Edmund Harrison to TJ, *PTJ*, 30 Dec. 1802.

53 Ibid.

54 A full listing of the known copies of the *Manual* is published in Brian Alexander and Madison Williams, *A Registry of Copies of Jefferson's* Manual *of 1801*, research memo (International Center for Jefferson Studies, 2021).

Rhode Island's first two U.S. senators, who served until 1803.[55]

Extending his reach abroad, Jefferson also provided the *Manual* to his admired correspondent, the French historian and philosopher Constantine Volney. In a letter from Washington, dated February 6, 1803, Jefferson was clear in hoping the work would serve his friend, who was then a senator in Napoleonic France: "As you are a member of a deliberative body, and might sometimes wish to know the rules of the oldest deliberative body we are acquainted with, I send you a copy of a Parliamentary Manual which I compiled for the use of the Senate, while I presided over them."[56] Modestly expressing his optimism of the *Manual*'s value to Volney, he added, "A bee will extract honey from any plant; so possibly may you from this."[57]

Judging by other evidence, Jefferson's *Manual* was met with continued demand. Bookseller catalogues list the *Manual* for sale in Albany, New York, in 1807, and a copy could be purchased for one dollar in Philadelphia in 1808.[58] In 1810, the 1801 edition was reprinted by publisher William Dickson in Lancaster, Pennsylvania.[59] When the Richmond bookseller

55 D.G.W., "The Hillhouse Collection," *The Yale University Library Gazette* 17, no. 3 (January 1943): 45–47 (possibly Donald G. Wing, Yale '26, listed in the Trustees of the Library); United States House of Representatives, "Hillhouse, James (1754–1832)," Biographical Directory of the United States Congress, bioguide.congress.gov/scripts/biodisplay.pl?index=H000618; Rhode Island Historical Society, "Theodore Foster Papers," Manuscripts Division (1997), www.rihs.org/mssinv/Mss424.htm.

56 TJ to Volney, *PTJ*, 6 Feb. 1803.

57 Ibid.

58 America's Historical Newspapers, "Advertisement," *Republican Crisis* (Albany, NY), vol. 1, issue 81, 18 Aug. 1807, 3; Early American Imprints, "Catalogue of Books Published by C. and A. Conrad & Co.," Philadelphia, 1808, 6.

59 Kevin J. Hays, *The Road to Monticello: The Life and Mind of Thomas Jefferson* (Oxford University Press, 2008), 527.

William Prichard requested additional copies from Jefferson in January 1811, he noted, "The great and daily enquiry among the Members of our Legislature for the Parliamentary Manuel of which Work there is not a Copy here to be had."[60] Later, after receiving the two dozen copies from Jefferson,[61] Prichard reiterated their popularity: "I have sold all the Parliamentary Manual save one."[62] Around this same time, copies were requested personally of Jefferson from David Bailie Warden, the Irish-born scholar and then aspiring American diplomat, who wanted one for himself as well as one "which I promised to send to a friend at Paris."[63] Serving in Paris a couple of years later, Warden wrote to Jefferson that the abdication of Napoleon "has occasioned an enquiry concerning parliamentary practise; and your manual, on this subject, has been sought by several Officers of the Government. no copy can be found here.—I hope soon to receive one from Philadelphia."[64]

Jefferson's Annotations as the Basis of the Second Edition

The story of the annotations in copies of the *Manual* provides evidence that Jefferson's intentions on the final word for the book lie not in the 1801 printing but in the second edition of 1812, which is reproduced in the volume the reader presently

60 William Prichard to TJ, *PTJRS*, 14 Jan. 1811. Along with these copies, Jefferson provided the the "little supplement" of additions (TJ to William Prichard, *PTJRS*, 6 Dec. 1810).

61 TJ to William Prichard, *Papers PTJRS*, 25 Jan. 1811.

62 William Prichard to TJ, *Papers PTJRS*, 16 Jul. 1812.

63 David Bailie Warden to TJ, *Papers PTJRS*, 16 Jan. 1811.

64 David Bailie Warden to TJ, *Papers PTJRS*, 6 May 1814.

holds in their hands. A decade after the *Manual* first appeared in print, Jefferson facilitated the publication of a new edition. In January 1812, Jefferson responded to the inquiries of the Georgetown publisher, Joseph Milligan, assenting to his request to publish a second edition of his *Manual*, writing: "I am perfectly willing that you should print another edition of the Parliamentary Manual."[65] In this letter, Jefferson revealed something of his further reading on parliamentary law, adding, "When I compiled it, I had never yet seen the 4th vol. of Hatsell. a subsequent perusal of that volume enabled me to make some useful additions which I had printed, & now inclose you a copy of them. these should be inserted in the text of the new edition in their proper places."[66] These "useful additions" are, in all likelihood, the lost printed supplement from 1806, as previously mentioned.

Jefferson also offered instructions to Milligan regarding the size of the new edition: "I wonder you should think of printing them in 8vo [octavo]. it is essentially a book for the pocket, & which members will carry to their house in their pocket occasionally, & some habitually. for this purpose I found it convenient to trim off all the margin of the former edition & reduce one of them to the size of 5. by 3."[67] This latter advice was evidently followed, as the edition published by Milligan on March 24, 1812, is markedly smaller and more pocket-sized than its predecessor.[68] The present edition, befitting more con-

65 TJ to Joseph Milligan, *PTJRS*, 7 Jan. 1812.

66 Ibid.

67 Ibid.

68 Interestingly, Library of Congress copy 3, presented to Trist on May 29, 1826, is an 1801 edition by Smith, but my physical inspection of it indicates it is trimmed

temporary tastes in publishing, closely matches the original octavo size of publisher Samuel Harrison Smith's 1801 edition.

The details of the handwritten annotations in copies of the 1801 *Manual* and Jefferson's clear instructions to the publisher Milligan to insert the new text are reflected in the second edition of 1812. Combined, this evidence indicates that the second edition reflects the most accurate and approved last word by Thomas Jefferson on the content of his *Manual.*

Jefferson's Lasting Standard

Writing to the publisher Joseph Milligan in 1812, in response to the question of the publication of a second edition of the *Manual,* Jefferson said, "If it can be made to promote order & decorum in debate it will do great good."[69] Jefferson understood the importance of parliamentary rules in the effective functioning of republican government. In order to see his political ideals function in practice, institutions would have to be up to the task. In writing the *Manual* in the first place, he was attempting to deliver on that promise. The careful annotations in the three copies of the *Manual* indicate that Jefferson as president took great care in continuing to reflect upon and

and bound to the smaller size. Exactly when this smaller binding was produced is unclear. Given Jefferson's wishes and the presence of this copy in his possession until near the end of his life, it suggests that Jefferson himself had it trimmed and bound in the smaller pocket size and, I surmise, the Library copy 3 is the copy Jefferson "found convenient to trim" that he referenced in his letter to Milligan. For additional narrative on the Milligan publication, see Howell, *Parliamentary Writings*, 31–36.

69 TJ to Milligan, Ibid.

advocate on behalf of his views of parliamentary law and its role in good governance. This effort, undertaken during the years of his presidency, formed the basis for the true second edition of the *Manual*, published in 1812. Not only did Jefferson continue to study parliamentary law, but he also put substantial effort into promoting his vision for it. The record of his correspondence, especially the two annotated copies he presented to leaders in the Virginia legislature, including the Holmes copy newly presented here, strongly points to his commitment to the subject.

However, in all the years for which Jefferson's *Manual* has served as a standard for the U.S. Congress, it has been the 1801 edition, not the second edition of 1812, that has been used. The *Manual* was formally adopted by the House of Representatives in the First Session of the Twenty-Fifth Congress by resolution, on September 15, 1837. The rule, which still exists,[70] was passed during the biannual deliberation on rules that occurs at the beginning of each Congress. When the House adopted the *Manual*, it selected, without apparent explanation, the first edition of 1801 rather than the second edition, which was published with Jefferson's input in 1812.

On Monday, September 4, 1837, eleven-term Representative Charles Fenton Mercer of Aldie, Virginia, serving then as a Whig, moved a resolution to form a committee to determine the rules and orders of proceeding of the House of the Twenty-Fifth Congress.[71] The committee was appointed on Thursday,

70 "Constitution, Jefferson's Manual, and Rules of the House of Representatives," 116th Congress, House Document 115–77 (2019): 127.

71 "House Journal, 25th Congress, 1st Session," U.S. Congressional Serial Set (1837), Thomas Allen, page 10 (September 4).

September 7, with eight days to report a rules proposal and composed of the following five members: Mr. Mercer, Thomas Lyon Hamer (Democrat of Georgetown, Ohio), George Nixon Briggs (Whig of Lanesboro, Massachusetts), Francis O.J. Smith (Democrat of Portland, Maine), and Henry A.P. Muhlenberg (Democrat of Reading, Pennsylvania).[72]

The select committee made its report on September 13, and debate on the proposed rules occurred over the next two days.[73] It was during debate on the adoption of the rules that Mr. Mercer reported a further amendment on September 15:

> The rules of parliamentary practice, comprised in Jefferson's Manual, shall govern the house in all cases to which they are applicable; and in which they are not inconsistent with the standing rules and orders of the House, and the joint rules of the Senate and House of Representatives.[74]

The House *Journal* states, "This amendment was read, and agreed to by the House."[75] Prior to this amendment, Jefferson's *Manual* had not been formally included in the rules of the House.

Upon adoption of the final rules package on September 15, it was ordered, on motion of Mr. Mercer, "that the rules be printed as amended; and that Jefferson's Manual of Parliamentary

---

72 "House Journal, 25th Congress, 1st Session," page 42 (September 7); Office of the House Historian, Biographical Directory of the United States Congress, 1774–Present, bioguideretro.congress.gov.

73 "House Journal, 25th Congress, 1st Session," page 54 (September 14).

74 "House Journal, 25th Congress, 1st Session," pages 62–63 (September 15).

75 Ibid, 63.

Practice be also printed with the rules."[76] On Monday, September 18, on motion of Representative John Quincy Adams, the former president then serving as a Whig from Massachusetts, it was ordered "that the edition of the Rules and Orders of the House, with Jefferson's Manual of Practice [*sic*], ordered to be printed on the 15th instant, consist of two thousand copies, and that the same be well bound."[77]

The record of these deliberations to incorporate Jefferson's *Manual* into the House rules is silent on which edition of the *Manual*, 1801 or 1812, should be used. However, in the two thousand "well bound" copies of the rules ordered published on the motion of Congressman Adams, it is the 1801 first edition of Jefferson's *Manual* that was printed.[78] Close inspection of the *Manual* published in the 1837 volume of House Rules reveals that it was based on the 1801 edition published by Samuel Harrison Smith. This claim is supported by the absence of all new paragraphs, other additional text, and all references to vol. 4 of John Hatsell's *Precedents of Proceedings in the House of Commons*, which are included in the 1812 second edition published by Joseph Milligan with Jefferson's input.

The esteemed late Senate Parliamentarian Floyd M. Riddick suggests that the 1812 edition should serve as the edition used by the Congress, rather than the 1801 edition as historically

---

76 Ibid, 64.

77 "House Journal, 25th Congress, 1st Session," page 65 (September 18).

78 United States, *Constitution of the United States of America: Rules of the House of Representatives, Joint Rules of the Two Houses, and Rules of the Senate, with Jefferson's Manual* (Thomas Allen, Printer to the House, 1837). Verso to the title page indicates "C. Sherman and Co., Printers, of 19 St. James Street, Philadelphia." A binder's mark on the rear endpaper indicates the edition was well bound by "Gaskill, Binder, No. 42 So. 5th St., Philad." (Author's personal copy.)

practiced. In a review of Wilber Samuel Howell's exhaustive work on Jefferson's parliamentary writings, Riddick stated, "There are a number of variations in contents and citations of Jefferson's *Manual* as printed in this volume compared to those printed in the Manual of the House of Representatives and the 1975 edition of the Senate Manual. These should be checked out and verified by someone, and if this version is absolutely correct, the House of Representatives might do well to replace its current version as printed in its Manual from Congress to Congress by substituting this one."[79]

I have responded to Riddick's call to be just that someone. As the evidence presented in this essay and in the text of the second edition of the *Manual* make clear, it is time to correct the historical error and to reflect Thomas Jefferson's intentions on the text of his *Manual*. The second edition, with the Last Additions of the Author, as presented in the present volume, should become the proper standard edition used by legislative bodies that rely on Jefferson's *Manual* for their rules and precedent. Indeed, the Parliamentarian of the House of Representatives has responded to this suggestion by incorporating the substantive changes and citations added by Jefferson in the second edition to the *House Rules and Manua*l printed for the 119th Congress in 2025.[80] More than 200 years after its publication in 1812, the second edition of Jefferson's *Manual* house found its place in the U.S. Congress. Other legislative bodies should follow suit.

79 Floyd M. Riddick, "Reviewed Works: Jefferson's Parliamentary Writings: 'Parliamentary Pocket-Book' and a Manual of Parliamentary Practice by Wilbur Samuel Howell," *Presidential Studies Quarterly* 19, no. 3 (674–75).

80 Ibid. U.S. House of Representatives 2025.

In a poignant coda to his long engagement with parliamentary law, in the last weeks of his life Jefferson presented a personal copy of the 1801 edition of the Manual to his grandson-in-law Nicholas P. Trist at Monticello. Inside the front cover, in what is likely Trist's handwriting, it states, "From Thomas Jefferson to N.P. Trist, Monticello, May 29, 1826."[81] Jefferson died just over a month later, on July 4. Jefferson's Manual, as reflective of his scholarship and his promotion of parliamentary law, is representative of his lifelong concern with institutions of government and the defense of individual liberty. The importance of rules in democratic legislatures endures. The Manual of Parliamentary Practice is, indeed, a lasting standard by which Thomas Jefferson can be judged.

81 See Library of Congress (copy 3), supra.

Editorial Method

The text of Jefferson's *Manual of Parliamentary Practice* printed here reflects what is best known of Jefferson's final intentions for the book. The main body of this edition was prepared based on a careful line-by-line transcription and comparison of three previously published editions: Samuel Harrison Smith, 1801 (Washington, D.C.); Joseph Milligan, 1812 (Georgetown); and Wilbur Samuel Howell, 1988 (Princeton). **Boldface** indicates additions of new text appearing in the 1812 second edition. Editorial notes explain variance between the Smith 1801 edition and the Milligan 1812 edition, as well as Jefferson's handwritten annotations in three copies of the 1801 Smith edition, herein referred to as the Library of Congress copy, the Brooke copy, and the Holmes copy. Notes also indicate variance from Howell's version (1988) to provide scholars and parliamentarians a consistent and reliable standard in the present edition that complements former authoritative editions of the book. Locations of Jefferson's handwritten annotations are provided by footnotes in this edition where they appear in the three physical copies of the 1801 edition. Typographical symbols such as the asterisk (*) or dagger (†) appear identically as they do in the 1812 Milligan text. Abbreviations and works cited are those of Jefferson, as they appear in the 1812 edition. These are not always consistent with one another, and no bibliography of references was provided in editions of the *Manual* published by Jefferson; for a list of works likely cited by Jefferson, the reader is referred to Howell, *Parliamentary Writings*, pages xv–xxvii. The index reproduces that published with Milligan's 1812 edition and implicitly receives Jefferson's imprimatur as it matches the index published in Smith (1801) without modification. The Milligan edition of 1812 was bound with copies of the U.S. Constitution and the contemporary rules of the House and Senate, although the 1801 Smith edition was not. Because Jefferson never indicated a preference on this point and such material is readily available from numerous sources, the Constitution and rules are not included in this edition.

Not every one of Jefferson's annotations warrants specific explanation, but several are worth highlighting for how they illustrate his ongoing scholarship, method, and intentions for the text of the *Manual*. For instance, Section 5, "Qualifications," of the 1801 Smith edition, contains a table of "apportionments of Representatives made in the constitution in 1787, and afterwards by Congress" (Para. 5.7). The table lists the sixteen states of the Union in early 1801; two completed columns listing the apportionments for 1787 and 1793, respectively; and one blank column for the year 1801, the first year for which new constitutionally-mandated decennial apportionments would be required. In the blank column under "1801" of both the Library and the Holmes copies, Jefferson wrote in by hand all of the apportionment figures for the corresponding states (fig 6.). Using the Holmes copy as evidence, we can therefore date Jefferson's annotations to Section 5 as sometime between March 1803, when Ohio became a state, and the date of the presentation to Holmes in December that year. Thus, Jefferson was marking up his *Manual* after the two-year point in the first term of his presidency.[82]

82 Jefferson's math on the table in the Library copy for columns 1 and 2 is correct.

A total of twenty-one annotations in the Library copy are stand-alone references to sections of Hatsell, vol. 4, made without any additional text or commentary, at places where Jefferson presumably observed that ideas from Hatsell's volume corresponded to his own previous writing. Stand-alone references to Hatsell occur only once in the Holmes copy and not at all in the pages of the Brooke copy. At least one annotation points to Jefferson's reading and research beyond Hatsell, where in Section 13, "Examination of Witnesses," a new reference to the second volume of Salmon and Emyln's eighteenth-century work on state trials appears (at Para. 13.1, "2 St. Tr. 588" in the Library copy).[83] The remaining annotations are additions of new text, ranging from short phrases to a few sentences. All of the annotations in the Brooke and Holmes copies appear in the Library copy, with the exception of minor variance between the apportionment tables in Section 5, "Qualifications," of the Holmes and the Library

---

The sum of 141 in the "1801" column apparently does not include the 1 for Ohio written below it, which would make the total 142. The handwritten figures in the "1801" column are identical in the Library and the Holmes copies. Wendell Ford notes, "Jefferson added these figures to his personal copy following the Census of 1800 and the admission of Ohio in 1803" (Wendell H. Ford in Thomas Jefferson, *A Manual of Parliamentary Practice for the Use of the Senate of the United States* [U.S. Government Printing Office, 1993], 13). We now know that Jefferson also added these figures to the Holmes copy, but other copies of the first edition once in Jefferson's hands exist without these figures added to them, including the non-annotated personal copy held by the Library of Congress (Copy 3), presented to N.P. Trist (see Library catalogue entry, KF4982 .J43 Copy 3).

83 Although Jefferson's Memorandum Books are insufficient in detail on when Jefferson acquired new works on parliamentary law during this time, a deeper search of the archives of invoices of booksellers and binders such as John March and J. Philippe Reibelt may reveal purchases of additional books on parliamentary law (Thomas Jefferson, *Jefferson's Memorandum Books: 1767–1826,* eds. James A. Bear and Lucia C. Stanton Jr. [Princeton University Press, 1997], 1057 fn. 26).

copies, some inconsequential differences in punctuation, one instance where he miswrote a date in a quotation from Hatsell, and an annotation on ratification in Section 52, "Treaties," which appears in the Brooke copy alone.[84]

Other annotations provide insights as well as questions about Jefferson's editorial intentions. For example, annotations in the earliest presentation copy, given by Jefferson to Brooke in December 1802, are limited to two sections, one in Section 22 on the reading of bills and the other in Section 52 on treaties. Each presents small puzzles. The former is an instance where Jefferson was inconsistent in his annotations; the latter is a case where he may have changed his mind. At Section 22, in the right margin of the Brooke copy, Jefferson wrote, "These words should be in Italics," referring to adjacent printed words underscored with a sequence of dots, "which readings shall be on three different days, unless the Senate unanimously direct otherwise" (Sec. 22, Para. 1). Howell writes of this as a case of "Smith's failure to conform to TJ's final manuscript" and Jefferson correcting his publisher, "trifling as it may seem."[85] In the 1812 second edition, Milligan corrects the words in question (see Milligan edition, 1812, 69). The same instruction appears at the same location in the Library copy. Curiously, however, the note is absent in the Holmes copy. Presumably this inconsistency was an oversight by Jefferson in annotating the Holmes copy, considering that

84 Jefferson's discrepancy in dates between the Library and Holmes copies is written at Sec. 26, "Bills, Commitment," paragraph 9. Hatsell writes of the precedent on April 24, 1626, at 4 Hats. 124 (Hatsell, *Precedents*, 1796), as in the Library copy, not the year 1606, as TJ wrote in the Holmes copy. In the 1812 Milligan edition, the correct year, 1626, is printed.

85 Howell, *Parliamentary Writings*, 339.

the Brooke copy was given away earlier and the Library copy was in his possession longer. What's more, later in the same paragraph in a handwritten note of the Library copy, but not the Brooke copy, Jefferson struck and replaced new text that was also underscored to be annotated, indicating continued attention to the newly italicized passage. That the annotations were written at least at the time of the gift to Brooke and later incorporated into the 1812 edition suggests that Jefferson did intend it in the revision and likely the original, even though he omitted these from the Holmes copy.

One annotation is exclusive to the Brooke copy. In Section 52, "Treaties," of the Brooke copy, at the end of the fourth paragraph of Section 52, a "+" is written, referencing the following note inscribed at the bottom of the page: "The treaty of the Pardo between Spain & G.B. in 1739. being disapproved by parliament, was not ratified, in consequence whereof the war it was intended to prevent took place. Observns of France on Memorial of England. pa. 107" (Sec. 52, Para. 4). Interestingly, this annotation does not appear in the Library or Holmes copies and is not included in the Milligan second edition. This is perhaps a printer's omission or, more arguably, between the time Jefferson was writing in the Brooke copy and making later edits, he either forgot or changed his mind about including that annotation. Howell includes the footnote in his edition in *Parliamentary Writings*, but with the caveat, "It should not be counted here, however, as an addition proposed by TJ for inclusion in Milligan's second edition,"[86] and it is included with the appropriate qualification in the edition printed here.

86 Howell, *Parliamentary Writings*, 432, ref. 420.

Regardless of Jefferson's intention, the Brooke copy contains an annotation by Jefferson that appears nowhere else.

The Library copy also contains fifteen Jefferson annotations that do not appear in Milligan's 1812 text. These are exclusively composed of new references to sections of Hatsell, vol. 4, which Jefferson apparently identified as correlating with text he had already written. It cannot be conclusively determined when Jefferson made these annotations or why they were not included in the 1812 second edition. Perhaps Jefferson did not find them significant enough to include in the second edition; perhaps they were not included in the printed supplement of additions he provided Milligan for the second edition; or it is possible he added them after that supplement was printed, as estimated, in 1806. Without additional information about the printed supplement or other evidence of the timing of Jefferson's additional reading, we are left to speculate. In any event, while the fifteen unpublished annotations are not substantial additions, they are included in the *Manual* printed in the present volume in their respective locations and noted as being exclusive to Jefferson's annotations in the Library copy. They are important in that Jefferson took care to write them, but the role he intended for them in the *Manual* itself remains, at present, an open question.

A MANUAL OF
PARLIAMENTARY
PRACTICE

A MANUAL

OF

PARLIAMENTARY PRACTICE:

FOR THE

USE OF THE SENATE

OF THE

UNITED STATES.

BY THOMAS JEFFERSON.

SECOND EDITION.

WITH THE LAST ADDITIONS OF THE AUTHOR.

WASHINGTON:

PUBLISHED BY WILLIAM COOPER; AND BY JOSEPH MILLIGAN, GEORGETOWN.

1812.

FIGURE 7 (previous). Title page to Jefferson's Manual, second edition, published by Joseph Milligan of Georgetown, 1812. Following Jefferson's suggestion, Milligan printed the second edition in a smaller size, approximately 3 inches by 5 inches, "which members will carry to their house in their pocket" (TJ to Milligan 7 January 1812).

TABLE OF CONTENTS.

TABLE OF CONTENTS.

PREFACE.

THE Constitution of the United States establishing a legislature for the Union, under certain forms, authorises each branch of it "to determine the rules of its own proceedings." The Senate have accordingly formed some rules for its own government: but these going only to few cases, they have referred to the decision of their President, without debate and without appeal, all questions of order arising either under their own rules, or where they have provided none. This places under the discretion of the President a very extensive field of decision, and one which, irregularly exercised, would have a powerful effect on the proceedings and determinations of the House. The President must feel weightily and seriously this confidence in his discretion; and the necessity of recurring, for its government, to some known system of rules, that he may neither leave himself free to indulge caprice or passion, nor open to the imputation of them. But to what system of rules is he to recur, as supplementary to those of the Senate? To this there can be but one answer; to the system of regulations adopted for the government of some one of the Parliamentary bodies within these states, or of that which has served as a prototype to most of them. This last is the model which we have all studied, while we are little acquainted with the modifications of it in our several states. It is deposited too in publications possessed by many and open to all. Its rules are probably as wisely constructed for governing the debates of a deliberative body, and obtaining its true sense, as any which can become known to us; and the acquiescence of the Senate, hitherto, under the references to them, has given them the sanction of their approbation.

Considering therefore the law of proceedings in the Senate as composed of the precepts of the Constitution, the regulations of the Senate, and, where these are silent, of the rules of Parliament, I have here endeavored to collect and digest so much of these as is called for in ordinary practice, collating the Parliamentary with the Senatorial rules, both where they agree and where they vary. I have done this, as well to have them at hand for my own government, as to deposit with the Senate the standard by which I judge and am willing to be judged. I could not doubt the necessity of quoting the sources of my information; among which Mr. Hatsell's most valuable book is pre-eminent; but as he has only treated some general heads, I have been obliged to recur to other authorities in support of a number of common rules of practice to which his plan did not descend. Sometimes each authority cited supports the whole passage. Sometimes it rests on all taken together. Sometimes the authority goes only to a part of the text, the residue being inferred from known rules and principles. For some of the most familiar forms, no written authority is, or can be quoted; no writer having supposed it necessary to repeat what all were presumed to know. The statement of these must rest on their notoriety.

I am aware that authorities can often be produced in opposition to the rules which I lay down as Parliamentary. An attention to dates will generally remove their weight. The proceedings of Parliament in antient times, and for a long while, were crude, multiform and embarrassing. They have been, however, constantly advancing towards uniformity and accuracy; and have now attained a degree of aptitude to their object, beyond which, little is to be desired or expected.

Yet I am far from the presumption of believing that I may not have mistaken the Parliamentary practice in some cases; and especially in those minor forms, which, being practised daily, are supposed known to every body, and therefore have not been committed to writing. Our resources, in this quarter of the globe, for obtaining information on that part of the subject, are not perfect. But I have begun a sketch, which those who come after me will successivelv correct and fill up, till a code of rules shall be formed for the use of the Senate, the effects of which may be, accuracy in business, economy of time, order, uniformity, and impartiality.

NOTE. The rules and practices peculiar to the *Senate* are printed in *Italic.*

Those of *Parliament* are in the Roman letter.

A MANUAL

OF

PARLIAMENTARY PRACTICE.

IMPORTANCE OF RULES.

Sec. I. THE IMPORTANCE OF ADHERING TO RULES.

MR. ONSLOW, the ablest among the Speakers of the House of Commons, used to say, 'it was a maxim he had often heard, when he was a young man, from old and experienced members, that nothing tended more to throw power into the hands of administration and those who acted with the majority of the House of Commons, than a neglect of, or departure from, the rules of proceeding: that these forms, as instituted by our ancestors, operated as a check and controul on the actions of the majority, and that they were in many instances, a shelter and protection to the minority, against the attempts of power.' So far the maxim is certainly true, and is founded in good sense, that as it is always in the power of the majority, by their numbers, to stop any improper measures proposed on the part of their opponents, the only weapons by which the minority can defend themselves against similar attempts from those in power, are the forms and rules of proceeding which have been adopted as they were found necessary from time to time, and are become the law of the House; by a strict adherence to which, the weaker party can only be protected from those irregularities and abuses which these forms were intended to check, and which the wantonness of power is but too often apt to suggest to large and successful majorities. 2 *Hats.* 171, 172.

And whether these forms be in all cases the most rational or not, is really not of so great importance. It is much more material that there should be a rule to go by, than what that rule is; that there may be an uniformity of proceeding in business, not subject to the caprice of the Speaker, or captiousness of the members. It is very material that order, decency and regularity, be preserved in a dignified public body. 2 *Hats.* 149.

And in 1698 the Lords say, "the reasonableness of what is desired is never considered by us, for we are bound to consider nothing but what is usual. Matters of form are essential to government, and 'tis of consequence to be in the right. All the reason for forms is custom, and the law of forms is practice; and reason is quite out of doors. Some particular customs may not be grounded on reason, and no good account can be given of them; and yet many nations are zealous for them; and Englishmen are as zealous as any others to pursue their old forms and methods." 4 *Hats.* 258.[1]

1 "And in 1698 the Lords... 4 *Hats.* 258" is a handwritten annotation added by Jefferson in Sec. 1 after Para. 2 in the Library of Congress copy 4 (hereafter "Library

SEC. II. LEGISLATURE.

ALL Legislative powers herein granted, shall be vested in a Congress of the United States, which shall consist of a Senate and House of Representatives. Constitution of the United States, Art. 1. Sec. 1.

The Senators and Representatives shall receive a compensation for their services, to be ascertained by law, and paid out of the Treasury of the United States. Constitution of the United States, Art. 1. Sec. 6.

For the powers of Congress, see the following Articles and Sections of the Constitution of the United States. I. 4. 7. 8. 9. II. 1. 2. III. 3. IV. 1. 3. 5. and all the amendments.

SEC. III. PRIVILEGE.

THE privileges of the members of Parliament, from small and obscure beginnings, have been advancing for centuries, with a firm and never yielding pace. Claims seem to have been brought forward from time to time, and repeated, till some example of their admission enabled them to build law on that example. We can only therefore state the point of progression at which they now are. It is now acknowledged, 1. That they are at all times exempted from question elsewhere for any thing said in their own house; that during the time of privilege, 2. Neither a member himself,* his wife, or his servants, (familiares

*Ord. of the H. of Com. 1663. July 16.

copy") and the Holmes copy of Samuel Harrison Smith's edition of the *Manual* (1801) and is printed in Joseph Milligan's second edition (1812).

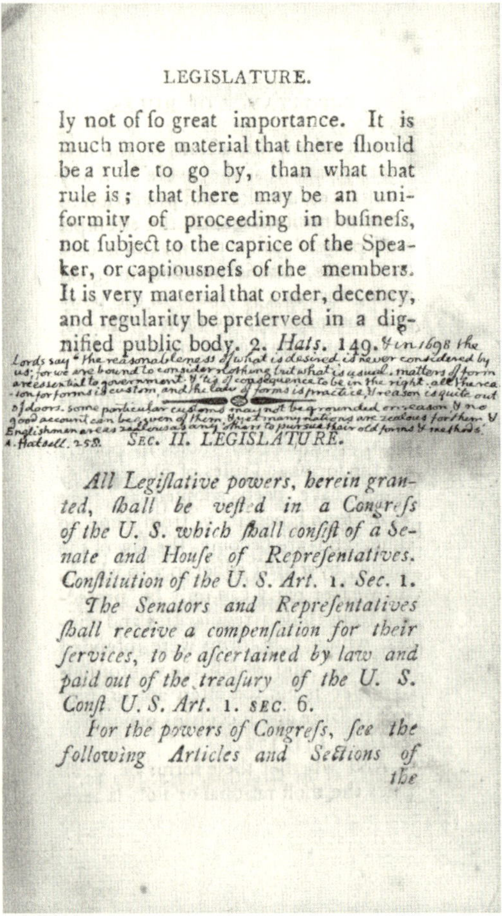

LEGISLATURE.

ly not of ſo great importance. It is much more material that there ſhould be a rule to go by, than what that rule is; that there may be an uniformity of proceeding in buſineſs, not ſubject to the caprice of the Speaker, or captiouſneſs of the members. It is very material that order, decency, and regularity be preſerved in a dignified public body. 2. *Hats.* 149. & in 1698 the Lords say "the reasonableness of what is desired is never considered by us; for we are bound to consider nothing but what is usual. matters of form are essential to government. & 'tis of consequence to be in the right. all the reason for forms is custom, and the law of forms is practice, & reason is quite out of doors. some particular customs may not be grounded on reason, & no good account can be given of them, & yet many nations are zealous for them & Englishmen are as zealous as any others to pursue their old forms & methods.' 4. Hatsell. 258.

SEC. II. LEGISLATURE.

All Legiſlative powers, herein granted, ſhall be veſted in a Congreſs of the U. S. which ſhall conſiſt of a Senate and Houſe of Repreſentatives. Conſtitution of the U. S. Art. 1. *Sec.* 1.

The Senators and Repreſentatives ſhall receive a compenſation for their ſervices, to be aſcertained by law and paid out of the treaſury of the U. S. Conſt. U. S. Art. 1. SEC. 6.

For the powers of Congreſs, ſee the following Articles and Sections of the

FIGURE 8. Jefferson's *Manual* (1801) (detail, Section 1), with annotations to the text by Jefferson, presented to Hugh Holmes, 22 December 1803.

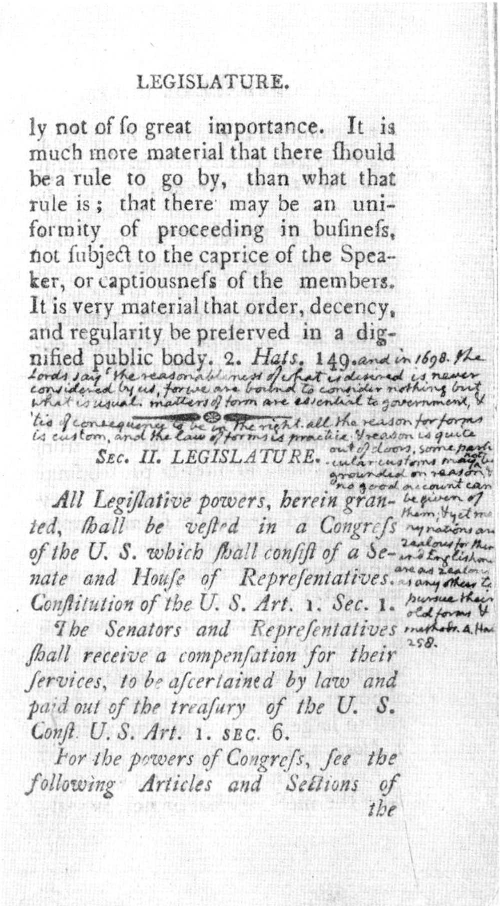

LEGISLATURE.

ly not of ſo great importance. It is much more material that there ſhould be a rule to go by, than what that rule is; that there may be an uniformity of proceeding in buſineſs, not ſubject to the caprice of the Speaker, or captiousneſs of the members. It is very material that order, decency, and regularity be preſerved in a dignified public body. 2. *Hats.* 149. and in 1698. the Lords say 'the reasonableness of what is desired is never considered by us, for we are bound to consider nothing but what is usual. matters of form are essential to government, & 'tis of consequence to be in the right. all the reason for forms is custom, and the law of forms is practice. & reason is quite out of doors. some particular customs may not be grounded on reason, & no good account can be given of them; & yet many nations are zealous for their and Englishmen are as zealous as any others to pursue their old forms & methods. 4. Hats. 258.

SEC. II. LEGISLATURE.

All Legiſlative powers, herein granted, ſhall be veſted in a Congreſs of the U. S. which ſhall conſiſt of a Senate and Houſe of Repreſentatives. Conſtitution of the U. S. Art. 1. *Sec.* 1.

The Senators and Repreſentatives ſhall receive a compenſation for their ſervices, to be aſcertained by law and paid out of the treaſury of the U. S. Conſt. U. S. Art. 1. SEC. 6.

For the powers of Congreſs, ſee the following Articles and Sections of the

FIGURE 9. Jefferson's *Manual* (1801) (detail, Section 1), with annotations to the text by Thomas Jefferson, Library of Congress.

sui) for any matter of their own, may be arrested,†[2] on mesne process, in any civil suit: 3. Nor be detained under execution, though levied before time of privilege: 4. Nor impleaded, cited, or subpœnaed in any court: 5. Nor summoned as a witness or juror: 6. Nor may their lands or goods be distrained: 7. Nor their persons assaulted, or characters traduced. And the period of time covered by privilege, before and after the session, with the practice of short prorogations under the connivance of the crown, amounts in fact to a perpetual protection against the course of justice. In one instance, indeed, it has been relaxed by the 10. G. 3. c. 50, which permits judiciary proceedings to go on against them. That these privileges must be continually progressive, seems to result from their rejecting all definition of them; the doctrine being that "their dignity and independence are preserved by keeping their privileges indefinite;" and that "the maxims upon which they proceed, together with the method of proceeding, rest entirely in their own breast, and are not defined and ascertained by any particular stated laws." 1. *Blackst.* 163. 164.[3]

It was probably from this view of the encroaching character of privilege, that the framers of our constitution, in their care to provide that the laws shall bind equally on all, and especially that those who make them shall not exempt themselves from their

† Elsynge 217. 1. Hats. 21.

2 Editor's note: In both Smith's 1801 and Milligan's 1812 editions of the *Manual*, a reference to "1. Grey's deb. 133." is included in the footnote along with Elsynge and Hatsell. Wilbur Samuel Howell persuasively argues that Jefferson did not intend for this reference to appear here, and thus it is excluded. See Howell, *Parliamentary Writings*, 427–28.

3 In the Library copy, Jefferson writes the annotation "4. Hats. 177 in note." at the end of Sec. 3., Para. 1. This does not appear in Milligan's 1812 edition.

operation, have only privileged "Senators and Representatives" themselves from the single act of "arrest in all cases, except treason, felony and breach of the peace, during their attendance at the session of their respective Houses, and in going to and returning from the same, and from being questioned in any other place for any speech or debate in either House." Const. U.S. Art. 1. Sec. 6. *Under the general authority "to make all laws necessary and proper for carrying into execution the powers given them,"* Const. U.S. Art. 2. Sec. 8., *they may provide by law the details which may be necessary for giving full effect to the enjoyment of this privilege. No such law being as yet made, it seems to stand at present on the following ground:* 1. *The act of arrest is void ab initio.** 2. *The member arrested may be discharged on motion.* 1. Bl. 166. 2. Stra. 990, *or by Habeas Corpus under the federal or state authority, as the case may be; or by a writ of privilege out of the Chancery,* 2 Stra. 989, *in those states which have adopted that part of the laws of England.* Orders of the H. of Commons. 1550. February 20. 3. *The arrest, being unlawful, is a trespass, for which the officer and others concerned are liable to action or indictment in the ordinary courts of justice, as in other cases of unauthorised arrest.* 4. *The court before which the process is returnable, is bound to act as in other cases of unauthorised proceeding, and liable also, as in other similar cases, to have their proceedings staid or corrected by the superior courts.*

The time necessary for going to and returning from Congress, not being defined, it will of course be judged of in every particular case by those who will have to decide the case.

While privilege was understood in England to extend, as it

*2. Stra. 989.

does here, only to exemption from arrest eundo, morando, et redeundo, the House of Commons themselves decided that "a convenient time was to be understood." (1580.) 1. *Hats.* 99, 100. Nor is the law so strict in point of time as to require the party to set out immediately on his return, but allows him time to settle his private affairs and to prepare for his journey; and does not even scan his road very nicely, nor forfeit his protection for a little deviation from that which is most direct; some necessity, perhaps, constraining him to it. 2. *Stra.* 986, 987.

This privilege from arrest, privileges of course against all process, the disobedience to which is punishable by an attachment of the person; as a subpœna ad respondendum, or testificandum, or a summons on a jury: and with reason; because a member has superior duties to perform in another place.

When a representative is withdrawn from his seat by summons, the 30,000 people whom he represents lose their voice in debate, and vote as they do on his voluntary absence: when a senator is withdrawn by summons, his state loses half its voice in debate and vote, as it does on his voluntary absence. The enormous disparity of evil admits no comparison.

So far, there will probably be no difference of opinion as to the privileges of the two Houses of Congress: but in the following cases it is otherwise. In December 1795, the H. of R. committed two persons of the name of Randall and Whitney, for attempting to corrupt the integrity of certain members, which they considered as a contempt and breach of the privileges of the House: and the facts being proved, Whitney was detained in confinement a fortnight, and Randall three weeks, and was reprimanded by the Speaker. In March 1796, the H. of R. voted a challenge given to a member of their House to be a breach of the privileges of the House; but satisfactory apologies and acknowledgments being made, no further proceeding was had. The editor of the Aurora having, in his paper of February 19, 1800, inserted some paragraphs defamatory of the Senate, and failed in his appearance, he was ordered to be committed. In debating the legality of this order, it was insisted, in support of it, that every man, by the law of nature, and every body of men, possesses the right of self defence; that all public functionaries are essentially invested with the powers of self-preservation; that they have an inherent right to do all acts necessary to keep themselves in a condition to discharge the trusts confided to them; that whenever authorities are given, the means of carrying them into execution are given by necessary implication; that thus we see the British Parliament exercise the right of punishing contempts; all the state legislatures exercise the same power; and every court does the same; that if we have it not, we sit at the mercy of every intruder, who may enter our doors or gallery, and, by noise, and tumult, render proceeding in business impracticable; that if our tranquillity is to be perpetually disturbed by newspaper defamation, it will not be possible to exercise our functions with the requisite coolness and deliberation; and that we must therefore have a power to punish these disturbers of our peace and proceedings. To this it was answered, that the Parliament and courts of England have cognisance of contempts by the express provisions of their law; that the state legislatures have equal authority, because their powers are plenary; they represent their constituents completely, and possess all their powers, except such as their constitutions have expressly denied them; that the courts of the several states have the same powers by the laws of their states, and those of the federal government by the same state laws, adopted in each state by a law of Congress; that none of these bodies therefore derive those powers from natural or necessary right, but from express law; that Congress have no such natural or necessary power, nor any powers but such as are given them by the constitution; that that has given them directly exemption from personal arrest, exemption from question elsewhere for what is said in their House, and power over their own members and proceedings; for these, no further law is necessary, the constitution being the law; that moreover, by that article of the constitution which authorises them "to make all laws necessary and proper for carrying into execution the powers vested by the constitution in them," they may provide by law for an undisturbed exercise of their functions, e.g. for the punishment of contempts, of affrays or tumult in their presence, &c. but, till the law be made, it does not exist; and does not exist, from their own neglect; that in the mean time, however, they are not unprotected, the ordinary magistrates and courts of law being open and competent to punish all unjustifiable disturbances or defamations, and even their own serjeant, who may appoint deputies ad libitum to aid him, 3 Grey. 59. 147. 255. *is equal to small disturbances; that in requiring a previous law, the constitution had regard to the inviolability of the citizen as well as of the member; as, should one House, in the regular form of a bill, aim at too broad privileges, it may be checked by the other, and both by the President; and also, as, the law being promulgated, the citizen will know how to avoid offence. But if one branch may assume its own privileges without controul, if it may do it on the spur of the occasion, conceal the law in its own breast, and, after the fact committed, make its sentence both the law and the judgment on that fact; if the offence is to be kept undefined, and to be declared only ex re nata, and according to the passions of the moment, and there be no limitation either in the manner or measure of the punishment, the condition of the citizen will be perilous indeed. Which of these doctrines is to prevail, time will decide. Where there is no fixed law, the judgment on any particular case is the law of that single case only, and dies with it. When a new and even a similar case arises, the judgment which is to make, and at the same time apply the law, is open to question and consideration, as are all new laws. Perhaps, Congress, in the mean time, in their care for the safety of the citizen, as well as that for their own protection, may declare by law what is necessary and proper to enable them to carry into execution the powers vested in them, and thereby hang up a rule for the inspection of all, which may direct the conduct of the citizen, and at the same time test the judgments they shall themselves pronounce in their own case.*

Privilege from arrest takes place by force of the election; and before a return be made, a member elected may be named of a committee, and is to every intent a member, except that he cannot vote until he is sworn. *Memor.* 107, 108. *Dewes* 642. *col.* 2, 643. *col.* 1. *Pet. Miscel. Parl.* 119. *Lex. Parl. c.* 23, 2. *Hats.* 22, 62.

Every man must, at his peril, take notice who are members of either House returned of record. *Lex. Parl.* 23, 4. *inst.* 24.

On complaint of a breach of privilege, the party may either be summoned, or sent for in custody of the serjeant. 1. *Grey,* 88, 95.

The privilege of a member is the privilege of the House. If the member waive it without leave, it is a ground for punishing him, but cannot in effect waive the privilege of the House. 3. *Grey* 140, 222.

For any speech or debate in either House, they shall not be questioned in any other place. *Const. U. S. I. 6. S. P. Protest of the Commons to James I.* 1621. 2. *Rapin, No.* 54. *pa.* 211, 212. But this is restrained to things done in the House in a Parliamentary course. 1. *Rush.* 663. For he is not to have privilege contra morem parliamentarium, to exceed the bounds and limits of his place and duty. *Com. P.*

If an offence be committed by a member in the House, of which the House has cognisance, it is an infringement of their right for any person or court to take notice of it, till the House has punished the offender, or referred him to a due course. *Lex. Parl.* 63.[4]

Privilege is in the power of the House, and is a restraint to the proceeding of inferior courts; but not of the House itself. 2. *Nalson* 450. 2. *Grey*, 399. For whatever is spoken in the House is subject to the censure of the House; and offences of this kind have been severely punished, by calling the person to the bar to make submission, committing him to the tower, expelling the House, &c. *Scob.* 72. *L. Parl. c.* 22.

It is a breach of order for the Speaker to refuse to put a question which is in order. 2. *Hats.* 175. 6. 5. *Grey* 133.

And even in cases of treason, felony, and breach of the peace, to which privilege does not extend as to substance, yet in Parliament, a member is privileged as to the mode of proceeding. The case is first to be laid before the House, that it may judge of the fact and of the grounds of the accusation, and how

4 Howell, *Parliamentary Writings*, italicizes this paragraph. It is not italicized in Smith's 1801 or Milligan's 1812 editions; Jefferson does not call for this to be italicized in his annotations; and the paragraph refers to conduct in the House of Representatives. Therefore, it is not italicized here.

far forth the manner of the trial may concern their privilege. Otherwise, it would be in the power of other branches of the government, and even of every private man, under pretences of treason, &c. to take any man from his service in the House, and so as many, one after another, as would make the House what he pleaseth. *Decl. of the Com. on the king's declaring Sir John Hotham a traitor.* 4. *Rushw.* 586. So when a member stood indicted of felony, it was adjudged that he ought to remain of the House till conviction. For it may be any man's case, who is guiltless, to be accused and indicted of felony, or the like crime. 23. *El.* 1580. *D'Ewes.* 283. *col. 1. Lex. Parl.* 133.

When it is found necessary for the public service to put a member under arrest, or when, on any public enquiry, matter comes out which may lead to affect the person of a member, it is the practice immediately to acquaint the House, that they may know the reasons for such a proceeding, and take such steps as they think proper. 2. *Hats.* 259. Of which see many examples. *Ib.* 256. 257. 258. But the communication is subsequent to the arrest. 1. *Blackst.* 167.

It is highly expedient, says Hatsell, for the due preservation of the privileges of the separate branches of the legislature, that neither should encroach on the other, or interfere in any matter depending before them, so as to preclude, or even influence that freedom of debate, which is essential to a free council. They are therefore not to take notice of any bills or other matters depending, or of votes that have been given, or of speeches which have been held, by the members of either of the other branches of the legislature, until the same have been communicated to them in the usual parliamentary manner. 2. *Hats.* 252.

4. *Inst.* 15. *Seld. Jud.* 53. Thus the king's taking notice of the bill for suppressing soldiers, depending before the House, his proposing a provisional clause for a bill before it was presented to him by the two Houses; his expressing displeasure against some persons for matters moved in Parliament during the debate and preparation of a bill, were breaches of privilege. 2. *Nalson*, 743. and in 1783, December 17, it was declared a breach of fundamental privileges, &c. to report any opinion or pretended opinion of the king on any bill or proceeding depending in either House of Parliament, with a view to influence the votes of the members. 2. *Hats.* 251, 6.

Sec. IV. ELECTIONS.

THE times, places, and manner of holding elections for Senators and Representatives, shall be prescribed in each state by the legislature thereof; but the Congress may, at any time, by law, make or alter such regulations, except as to the places of chusing Senators. Constitution I. 4.

Each House shall be the judge of the elections, returns, and *qualifications of its own members.* Constitution I. 5.

Sec. V. QUALIFICATIONS.

THE Senate of the United States shall be composed of two Senators from each state, chosen by the legislature thereof, for six years, and each Senator shall have one vote.

Immediately after they shall be assembled in consequence of the first election, they shall be divided as equally as may be into three classes. The seats of the Senators of the 1st class shall be vacated at the end of the 2d year; of the 2d class at the expiration of the 4th year; and of the 3d class at the expiration of the 6th year; so that one third may be chosen every second year; and if vacancies happen by resignation or otherwise, during the recess of the legislature of any state, the executive thereof may make temporary appointments, until the next meeting of the legislature, which shall then fill such vacancies.

No person shall be a Senator, who shall not have attained to the age of thirty years, and been nine years a citizen of the United States, and who shall not, when elected, be an inhabitant of that state for which he shall be chosen. Constitution I. 3.

The House of Representatives shall be composed of members chosen every second year by the people of the several states; and the electors in each state shall have the qualifications requisite for electors of the most numerous branch of the state legislature.

No person shall be a Representative who shall not have attained to the age of twenty-five years, and been seven years a citizen of the United States, and who shall not, when elected, be an inhabitant of that state in which he shall be chosen.

Representatives and direct taxes shall be apportioned among the several states which may be included within this Union, according to their respective numbers, which shall be determined by adding to the whole number of free persons, including those bound to service for a term of years, and including Indians not taxed, three fifths of all other persons.[5] *The actual enumeration shall be*

5 Jefferson misquotes the U.S. Constitution here, where the phrase "including Indians

made within three years after the first meeting of the Congress of the United States, and within every subsequent term of ten years, in such manner as they shall be law direct. The number of Representatives shall not exceed one for every thirty thousand, but each state shall have at least one Representative. Constitution of the United States I. 2.

The provisional apportionments of Representatives made in the constitution in 1787, and afterwards by Congress, were as follows:[6]

	1787	1793	1801	**1813**
New Hampshire,	3	4	**5**	**6**
Massachusetts,	8	14	**17**	**20**
Rhode Island,	1	2	**2**	**2**
Connecticut,	5	7	**7**	**7**
Vermont,		2	**6**	**6**
New-York,	6	10	**17**	**27**
Jersey,	4	5	**6**	**6**
Pennsylvania,	8	13	**18**	**23**
Delaware,	1	1	**1**	**2**
Maryland,	6	8	**9**	**9**
Virginia,	10	19	**22**	**23**
Kentucky,		2	**3**	**10**
Tennessee,			**1**	**6**
N. Carolina,	5	10	**12**	**13**
S. Carolina,	5	6	**8**	**9**
Georgia,	3	2	**4**	**6**
Ohio,				**6**

not taxed" should read "excluding Indians not taxed," as it appears in Article I, Section 2, Clause 3. This error appears in both the 1801 and 1812 editions and is not corrected in any of Jefferson's annotated copies. The editor thanks Endrina Tay and J. Jefferson Looney of Monticello's Robert H. Smith International Center for Jefferson Studies and Professor Marvin Langsam of Miami-Dade College (ret.) for noting the error.

6 In Smith's 1801 edition, the apportionment column for the year 1801 was printed blank. In the Library copy and the Holmes copy, Jefferson added apportionment

When vacancies happen in the representation from any state, the executive authority thereof shall issue writs of election to fill such vacancies. Constitution I. 2.

No Senator or Representative shall, during the time for which he was elected, be appointed to any civil office under the authority of the United States which shall have been created, or the emoluments whereof shall have been increased, during such time; and no person holding any office under the United States, shall be a member of either House during his continuance in office. Constitution I. 6.

SEC. VI. QUORUM.

A MAJORITY of each House shall constitute a quorum to do business: but a smaller number may adjourn from day to day, and may be authorised to compel the attendance of absent members, in such manner, and under such penalties as each House may provide. Constitution I. 5.

In general, the chair is not to be taken till a quorum for business is present; unless, after due waiting, such a quorum be despaired of; when the chair may be taken and the House adjourned. And whenever, during business, it is observed that a quorum is not present, any member may call for the House to be counted, and being found deficient, business is suspended. 2. *Hats.* 125. 126.

The President having taken the chair, and a quorum being present, the journal of the preceding day shall be read, to the end

---

figures under 1801 and, at the bottom of the table, a new row for Ohio. In the Library copy, Jefferson wrote the sums of the total number of representatives for each column. In Milligan's 1812 edition, a row for Ohio is added and apportionment figures are updated to include the totals for 1813.

that any mistake may be corrected that shall have been made in the entries. Rules of Senate 1.

SEC. VII. CALL OF THE HOUSE.

ON a call of the House, each person rises up as he is called, and answereth. The absentees are then only noted, but no excuse to be made till the House be fully called over. Then the absentees are called a second time, and if still absent, excuses are to be heard. *Ord. H. Com.* 92.

They rise that their persons may be recognized; the voice, in such a crowd, being an insufficient verification of their presence. But in so small a body as the Senate of the United States, the trouble of rising cannot be necessary.

Orders for calls on different days may subsist at the same time. 2. *Hats.* 72.

SEC. VIII. ABSENCE.

NO member shall absent himself from the service of the Senate, without leave of the Senate first obtained. And in case a less number than a quorum of the Senate shall convene, they are hereby authorised to send the serjeant at arms, or any other person or persons by them authorised, for any or all absent members, as the majority of such members present shall agree, at the expense of such absent members respectively, unless such excuse for non-attendance shall be made, as the Senate, when a quorum is convened, shall judge sufficient: and in that case, the expense shall be paid out of the contingent fund. And this rule shall apply as well to the first convention of Senate, at the legal time of meeting, as to each day of the session, after the hour is arrived to which the Senate stood adjourned. Rule 19.

Sec. IX. SPEAKER.

THE Vice-President of the United States shall be President of the Senate, but shall have no vote, unless they be equally divided. Constitution I. 3.

The Senate shall chuse their other officers, and also a President pro tempore, in the absence of the Vice-President, or when he shall exercise the office of President of the United States. Constitution I. 3.[7]

The House of Representatives shall chuse their Speaker and other officers. Constitution I. 2.

When but one person is proposed, and no objection made, it has not been usual in Parliament to put any question to the House; but without a question, the members proposing him conduct him to the chair. But if there be objection, or another proposed, a question is put by the clerk. 2. *Hats.* 158. As are also questions of adjournment. 6 *Grey.* 406. Where the House debated and exchanged messages and answers with the king for a week, without a Speaker, till they were prorogued. They have done it de diem in diem for fourteen days. 1. *Chand.* 331. 335.

In the Senate, a President pro tempore in the absence of the Vice-President is proposed, and chosen by ballot. His office is understood to be determined on the Vice-President's appearing and taking the chair, or at the meeting of the Senate after the first recess.

---

7 Howell (1988) excludes this paragraph, perhaps a typographical error, but it appears in Smith's 1801 and Milligan's 1812 editions.

Where the Speaker has been ill, other Speakers pro tempore have been appointed. Instances of this are 1. *H.* 4. Sir John Cheyney, and so Sir William Sturton, and in 15. *H.* 6. Sir John Tyrrel, in 1656, January 27. 1658, March 9. 1659, January 13.

Sir Job Charlton ill. Seymour chosen, 1673, February 18. Seymour being ill, Sir Robt. Sawyer chosen, 1678, April 15. Sawyer being ill, Seymour chosen.[8]	Not merely pro tem. 1 *Chand.* 169. 276, 277.

Thorpe in execution, a new Speaker chosen, 31 *H. VI.* 3 *Grey* 11. and March 14, 1694, Sir John Trevor chosen.[9] There have been no later instances 2 *Hats.* 161. 4 inst. 8 *L. Parl.* 263.

A Speaker may be removed at the will of the House and a Speaker pro tempore appointed. 2 *Grey* 186. 5 *Grey* 134.

Sec. X. ADDRESS.

THE President shall from time to time give to the Congress information of the state of the Union, and recommend to their consideration such measures as he shall judge necessary and expedient. Constitution II. 3.

8 In the Library copy, Jefferson adds "4. Hats. 29." adjacent to the text "Seymour chosen," which does not appear in Milligan's 1812 edition.

9 In Jefferson's Parliamentary Pocket-Book and Smith's 1801 edition of the *Manual*, the reference is to "31 H. VI." In Milligan's 1812 edition, "3 H. VI." is printed. It appears that Milligan made an error that Howell duplicated (see Howell pp. 160 and 367). It is corrected here.

A joint address of both Houses of Parliament is read by the Speaker of the House of Lords. It may be attended by both Houses in a body, or by a committee from each House, or by the two Speakers only. An address of the House of Commons only, may be presented by the whole House, or by the Speaker, 9 *Grey* 473. 1 *Chandler*, 298, 301. or by such particular members as are of the Privy Council. 2 *Hats.* 278.

SEC. XI. COMMITTEES.

STANDING committees, as of privileges and elections, &c. are usually appointed at the first meeting, to continue through the session. The person first named is generally permitted to act as chairman. But this is a matter of courtesy; every committee having a right to elect their own chairman, who presides over them, puts questions, and reports their proceedings to the House. 4 inst. 11, 12, *Scob.* 9. 1 *Grey* 122.

At these committees the members are to speak standing, and not sitting: though there is reason to conjecture it was formerly otherwise. *D'Ewes* 630. *col.* 1. 4. *Parl. Hist.* 440. 2 *Hats.* 77.

Their proceedings are not to be published, as they are of no force till confirmed by the House. *Rushw. Parl.* 3. *vol.* 2. 74. 3 *Grey* 401. *Scob* 39. Nor can they receive a petition but through the House. 9 *Grey* 412.

When a committee is charged with an enquiry, if a member prove to be involved, they cannot proceed against him, but must make a special report to the House, whereupon the member is heard in his place, or at the bar, or a special authority is given to the committee to enquire concerning him. 9 *Grey* 523.

So soon as the House sits, and a committee is notified of it, the chairman is in duty bound to rise instantly, and the members to attend the service of the House. 2 *Nals.* 319.

It appears that on joint committees of the Lords and Commons, each committee acted integrally in the following instances. 7 *Grey* 261, 278, 285, 338. 1 *Chandler* 357, 462. In the following instances it does not appear whether they did or not. 6 *Grey* 129. 7 *Grey* 213, 229, 321.

Sec. XII. COMMITTEE OF THE WHOLE.

THE speech, messages and other matters of great concernment, are usually referred to a committee of the whole House. 6 *Grey* 311. Where general principles are digested in the form of resolutions, which are debated and amended till they get into a shape which meets the approbation of a majority. These being reported and confirmed by the House, are then referred to one or more select committees, according as the subject divides itself into one or more bills. *Scob.* 36, 44. Propositions for any charge on the people are especially to be first made in a committee of the whole. 3 *Hats.* 127. The sense of the whole is better taken in committee, because in all committees every one speaks as often as he pleases. *Scob.* 49. They generally acquiesce in the chairman named by the Speaker: but, as well as all other committees, have a right to elect one, some member, by consent, putting the question. *Scob.* 36. 3 *Grey* 301. The form of going from the House into committee, is, for the Speaker, on motion, to put the question that the House do now resolve itself into a committee of the whole, to take under consideration such a matter, naming it. If determined in the affirmative, he leaves the chair, and takes a seat elsewhere, as any other member; and the person appointed chairman seats himself at the clerk's table. *Scob. 36.* Their quorum is the same as that of the House; and if a defect happens, the chairman, on a motion and question, rises, the Speaker resumes the chair, and the chairman can make no other report than to inform the House of the cause of their dissolution. If a message is announced during a committee, the Speaker takes the chair, and receives it, because the committee cannot. 2 *Hats.* 125, 126.

In a committee of the whole, the tellers on a division, differing as to the numbers, great heats and confusion arose, and danger of a decision by the sword. The Speaker took the chair, the mace was forcibly laid on the table, whereupon, the members retiring to their places, the Speaker told the House "he had taken the chair without an order, to bring the House into order." Some excepted against it; but it was generally approved as the only expedient to suppress the disorder. And every member was required, standing up in his place, to engage that he would proceed no further in consequence of what had happened in the grand committee, which was done. 3 *Grey* 128.

A committee of the whole being broken up in disorder, and the chair resumed by the Speaker without an order, the House was adjourned. The next day the committee was considered as thereby dissolved, and the subject again before the House; and it was decided in the House, without returning into committee. 3 *Grey* 130.

No previous question can be put in a committee; nor can this committee adjourn as others may; but if their business is unfinished, they rise, on a question, the House is resumed, and the chairman reports that the committee of the whole have, according to order, had under their consideration such a matter and have made progress therein; but not having had time to go through the same, have directed him to ask leave to sit again. Whereupon a question is put on their having leave, and on the time when the House will again resolve itself into a committee. *Scob.* 38. But if they have gone through the matter referred to them, a member moves that the committee may rise, and the chairman report their proceedings to the House; which being resolved, the chairman rises, the Speaker resumes the chair, the chairman informs him that the committee have gone through the business referred to them, and that he is ready to make report when the House shall think proper to receive it. If the House have time to receive it, there is usually a cry of "now, now," whereupon he makes the report: but if it be late, the cry is "to-morrow, to-morrow," or "on Monday, &c," or a motion is made to that effect, and a question put that it be received to-morrow, &c. *Scob.* 38.

In other things the rules of proceeding are to be the same as in the House. *Scob.* 39.

SEC. XIII. EXAMINATION OF WITNESSES.

COMMON fame is a good ground for the House to proceed by enquiry, and even to accusation. *Resolution House Commons* 1. *Car.* 1. 1625. *Rush. L. Parl.* 115. 1 *Grey* 16....22. 92. 8 *Grey* 21, 23, 27, 45.

As the heads of impeachment were severally read against the Lord Clarendon in 1667, some member in his place, stated to the House, "that several persons had undertaken to make that head good." Or, "that the member had heard this from a certain great lord." Or, "that this was too public to stand in need of proof." Or, in one instance, "that the member did not doubt that it will be made out." *St. Tr.* 558. 4 *Hats.* 137.[10]

Witnesses are not to be produced but where the House has previously instituted an enquiry. 2 *Hats.* 102. nor then are orders for their attendance given blank. 3 *Grey* 51. **The process is a summons from the House. 4. *Hats.* 255, 258.**[11]

When any person is examined before a committee, or at the bar of the House, any member wishing to ask the person a question, must address it to the Speaker or Chairman, who repeats the question to the person, or says to him, "you hear the question, answer it." But if the propriety of the question be objected to, the Speaker directs the witness, counsel and parties, to withdraw; for no question can be moved or put, or debated while they are there. 2 *Hats.* 108. Sometimes the questions are previously settled in writing before the witness enters. *Ib.* 106, 107. 8 *Grey* 64. The questions asked must be entered in the Journals. 3 *Grey* 81. But the testimony given in answer before the House is never written down; but before a committee it must be, for the information of the House, who are not present to hear it. 7 *Grey* 52, 334.

10 "As the heads... 4 *Hats.* 137" is an annotation by Jefferson at the end of Sec. 13, Para. 1 in the Library copy, which is printed in Milligan's 1812 edition. The reference in Jefferson's annotation in the Library copy is to "2 St. Tr. 588," but it is printed as "St. Tr. 588" in Milligan's 1812 edition.

11 "The process is... 4 *Hats.* 255, 258" is an annotation by Jefferson at the end of Sec. 13, Para. 3 in the Library copy, which is printed in Milligan's 1812 edition.

If either House have occasion for the presence of a person in custody of the other, they ask the other their leave that he may be brought up to them in custody. 3 *Hats.* 52.

A member, in his place, gives information to the House of what he knows of any matter under hearing at the bar. *Jour. H. of C. January* 22, 1744 .... 5.

Either House may request, but not command the attendance of a member of the other. They are to make the request by message to the other House, and to express clearly the purpose of attendance, that no improper subject of examination may be tendered to him. The House then gives leave to the member to attend, if he chuse it; waiting first to know from the member himself whether he chuses to attend, till which, they do not take the message into consideration. But when the peers are sitting as a court of criminal judicature, they may order attendance; unless where it be a case of impeachment by the Commons. There it is to be a request. 3 *Hats.* 17. 9 *Grey* 306, 406. 10 *Grey* 133.

Counsel are to be heard only on private, not on public bills, and on such points of law only as the House shall direct. 10 *Grey* 61.

Sec. XIV. ARRANGEMENT OF BUSINESS.

THE Speaker is not precisely bound to any rules as to what bills or other matter shall be first taken up, but is left to his own discretion, unless the House on a question decide to take up a particular subject. *Hakew.* 136.

A settled order of business is, however, necessary for the government of the presiding person, and to restrain individual members from calling up favorite measures, or matters under their special patronage, out of their just turn. It is useful also for directing the discretion of the House, when they are moved to take up a particular matter, to the prejudice of others having priority of right to their attention in the general order of business.

In Senate, the bills and other papers which are in possession of the House, and in a state to be acted on, are arranged every morning, and brought on in the following order.

1. Bills ready for a second reading are read, that they may be referred to committees, and so be put under way. But if, on their being read, no motion is made for commitment, they are then laid on the table in the general file, to be taken up in their just turn.

2. After twelve o'clock, bills ready for it are put on their passage.

3. Reports in possession of the House, which offer grounds for a bill, are to be taken up, that the bill may be ordered in.

4. Bills or other matters before the House and unfinished on the preceding day, whether taken up in turn, or on special order, are entitled to be resumed and passed on through their present stage.

5. These matters being dispatched, for preparing and expediting business, the general file of bills and other papers is then taken up, and each article of it is brought on according to its seniority, reckoned by the date of its first introduction to the House. Reports on bills belong to the dates of their bills.

In this way we do not waste our time in debating what shall be taken up: we do one thing at a time; follow up a subject while it is fresh, and till it is done with; clear the House of business gradatim as it is brought on, and prevent, to a certain degree, its immense accumulation towards the close of the session.

Arrangement however can only take hold of matters in possession of the House. New matter may be moved at any time, when no question is before the House. Such are original motions, and reports on bills. Such are bills from the other House, which are received at all times, and receive their first reading as soon as the question then before the House is disposed of; and bills brought in on leave, which are read first whenever presented. So messages from the other House respecting amendments to bills, are taken up as soon as the House is clear of a question, unless they require to be printed, for better consideration. Orders of the day may be called for, even when another question is before the House.

Sec. XV. ORDER.

EACH House may determine the rules of its proceedings; punish its members for disorderly behaviour, and, with the concurrence of two thirds, expel a member. Constitution I. 5.

In Parliament "instances make order" per Speaker Onslow, 2 *Hats.* 141. but what is done only by one Parliament, cannot be called custom of Parliament, by Prynne. 1 *Grey* 52.

Sec. XVI. ORDER RESPECTING PAPERS.

THE clerk is to let no journals, records, accounts, or papers be taken from the table, or out of his custody. 2 *Hats.* 193, 194.

Mr. Prynne having at a committee of the whole amended a mistake in a bill without order or knowledge of the committee, was reprimanded. 1 *Chand.* 77.

A bill being missing, the House resolved that a protestation should be made and subscribed by the members "before Almighty God and this honorable House, that neither myself nor any other to my knowledge, have taken away, or do at this present conceal a bill entitled, &c." 5 *Grey* 202.

After a bill is engrossed, it is put into the Speaker's hands, and he is not to let anyone have it to look into. *Town. col.* 209.

SEC. XVII. ORDER IN DEBATE.

WHEN the Speaker is seated in his chair, every member is to sit in his place. *Scob.* 6. 3 *Grey* 403.

When any member means to speak, he is to stand up in his place, uncovered, and to address himself, not to the House, or any particular member, but to the Speaker, who calls him by his name, that the House may take notice who it is that speaks. *Scob.* 6. *D'Ewes* 487. *Col.* 1. 2 *Hats.* 77. 4 *Grey* 66. 8 *Grey* 108. But members who are indisposed may be indulged to speak sitting. 2 *Hats.* 75, 77. 1 *Grey* 195.

In Senate, every member, when he speaks, shall address the chair, standing in his place, and when he has finished shall sit down. Rule 3.

When a member stands up to speak, no question is to be put, but he is to be heard, unless the House overrule him. 4 *Grey* 390. 5 *Grey* 6, 143.

If two or more rise to speak nearly together, the Speaker determines who was first up, and calls him by name, whereupon he proceeds, unless he voluntarily sits down and gives way to the other. But sometimes the House does not acquiesce in the Speaker's decision, in which case the question is put "which member was first up?" 2 *Hats.* 76. *Scob.* 7. *D'Ewes* 434. *col.* 1, 2.

In the Senate of the United States, the President's decision is without appeal. Their rule is in these words: When two members rise at the same time, the President shall name the person to speak; but in all cases, the member first rising, shall speak first. Rule 5.

No man may speak more than once to the same bill on the same day; or even on another day if the debate be adjourned. But if it be read more than once in the same day, he may speak once at every reading. *Co.* 12, 116. *Hakew.* 148. *Scob.* 58. 2 *Hats.* 75. Even a change of opinion does not give a right to be heard a second time. *Smyth Comw. L.* 2. *c.* 3. *Arcan. Parl.* 17.

The corresponding rule of Senate is in these words: No member shall speak more than twice in any one debate on the same day, without leave of the Senate. Rule 4.

But he may be permitted to speak again to clear a matter of fact. 3 *Grey* 357, 416. Or merely to explain himself, 2 *Hats.* 73. in some material part of his speech, *ib.* 75. or to the manner or words of the question, keeping himself to that only and not travelling into the merits of it; *Memorials in Hakew.* 29. or to the orders of the House if they be transgressed, keeping within that line, and not falling into the matter itself. *Mem. in Hakew.* 30, 31.

But if the Speaker rises to speak, the member standing up ought to sit down, that he may be first heard. *Town col.* 205. *Hale Parl.* 133. *Mem. in Hakew.* 30, 31. Nevertheless, though the Speaker may of right speak to matters of order and be first heard, he is restrained from speaking on any other subject, except where the House have occasion for facts within his knowledge; then he may, with their leave, state the matter of fact. 3 *Grey* 38.

No one is to speak impertinently or beside the question, superfluously or tediously. *Scob.* 31, 33. 2 *Hats.* 166, 168. *Hale Parl.* 133.

No person is to use indecent language against the proceedings of the House, no prior determination of which is to be reflected on by any member, unless he means to conclude with a motion to rescind it. 2 *Hats.* 169, 170. *Rushw. P.* 3. *v.* 1. *fol.* 42. But while a proposition is under consideration, is still in fieri, though it has even been reported by a committee, reflections on it are no reflections on the House. 9 *Grey* 508.

No person in speaking, is to mention a member then present by his name; but to describe him by his seat in the House, or who spoke last, or on the other side of the question, &c. *Mem. in Hakew.* 3 *Smyth's Comw. L.* 2. *c.* 3. nor to digress from the matter to fall upon the person, *Scob.* 31. *Hale Parl.* 133. 2 *Hats.* 166. by speaking reviling, nipping, or unmannerly words against a particular member. *Smyth's Comw. L.* 2. *c.* 3. The consequences of a measure may be reprobated in strong terms; but to arraign the motives of those who propose or advocate it, is a personality, and against order. Qui digreditur a materia ad personam, Mr. Speaker ought to suppress. *Ord. Com.* 1604. *Apr.* 19.

When a member shall be called to order, he shall sit down until the President shall have determined whether he is in order or not. Rule 16.[12]

12 This rule, an apparent reference to the Senate, would seemingly be italicized, but it is not italicized in Smith's 1801 edition or Milligan's 1812 edition, and Jefferson's annotations do not state that it should be italicized. See Howell, *Parliamentary Writings*, page 429, for additional discussion on this point.

No member shall speak to another, or otherwise interrupt the business of the Senate, or read any printed paper while the Journals or public papers are reading, or when any member is speaking in any debate. Rule 2.

No one is to disturb another in his speech by hissing, coughing, spitting, 6 *Grey* 332. *Scob.* 8. *D'Ewes* 332. *col.* 1. 640. *col.* 2. speaking or whispering to another; *Scob.* 6. *D'Ewes.* 487. *col.* 1. nor to stand up or interrupt him; *Town. col.* 205. *Mem. in Hakew.* 31. nor to pass between the Speaker and the speaking member, nor to go across the House; *Scob.* 6. or to walk up and down it, or to take books or papers from the table, or write there. 2 *Hats.* 171.

Nevertheless, if a member finds that it is not the inclination of the House to hear him, and that by conversation or any other noise they endeavour to drown his voice, it is his most prudent way to submit to the pleasure of the House, and sit down; for it scarcely ever happens that they are guilty of this piece of ill manners without sufficient reason, or inattentive to a member who says any thing worth their hearing. 2 *Hats.* 77, 78.

If repeated calls do not produce order, the Speaker may call by his name any member obstinately persisting in irregularity, whereupon the House may require the member to withdraw. He is then to be heard in exculpation, and to withdraw. Then the Speaker states the offence committed, and the House considers the degree of punishment they will inflict. 2 *Hats.* 167, 7, 8, 172.

For instances of assaults and affrays in the House of Commons, and the proceedings thereon, see 1. *Pet. Misc.* 82. 3 *Grey* 128. 4 *Grey* 328. 5 *Grey* 382. 6 *Grey* 254. 10 *Grey* 8. Whenever warm words, or an assault, have passed between members, the House, for the protection of their members, requires them to declare in their places not to prosecute any quarrel; 3 *Grey* 128, 293. 5 *Grey* 289. or orders them to attend the Speaker, who is to accommodate their differences and report to the House: 3 *Grey* 419. and they are put under restraint if they refuse, or until they do. 9 *Grey* 234, 312.

Disorderly words are not to be noticed till the member has finished his speech. 5 *Grey* 356. 6 *Grey* 60. Then the person objecting to them, and desiring them to be taken down by the clerk at the table, must repeat them. The Speaker then may direct the clerk to take them down in his minutes. But if he thinks them not disorderly, he delays the direction. If the call becomes pretty general, he orders the clerk to take them down, as stated by the objecting member. They are then part of his minutes, and when read to the offending member, he may deny they were his words, and the House must then decide by a question whether they are his words or not. Then the member may justify them, or explain the sense in which he used them, or apologize. If the House is satisfied, no farther proceeding is necessary. But if two members still insist to take the sense of the House, the member must withdraw, before that question is stated, and then the sense of the House is to be taken. 2 *Hats.* 199. 4 *Grey* 170. 6 *Grey* 59. When any member has spoken, or other business intervened after offensive words spoken, they cannot be taken notice of for censure. And this is for the common security of all, and to prevent mistakes which must happen if words are not taken down immediately. Formerly they might be taken down any time the same day. 2 *Hats.* 196. *Mem. in Hakew.* 71. 3 *Grey* 48. 9 *Grey* 514.

Disorderly words spoken in a committee must be written down as in the House; but the committee can only report them to the House for animadversion. 6 *Grey* 46.

The rule of the Senate says, if a member be called to order for words spoken, the exceptionable words shall be immediately taken down in writing, that the President may be better enabled to judge. Rule 17.

In Parliament, to speak irreverently or seditiously against the king is against order. *Smyth's Comw. L.* 2. *c.* 3. 2 *Hats.* 170.

It is a breach of order in debate to notice what has been said on the same subject in the other House, or the particular votes or majorities on it there: because the opinion of each House should be left to its own independency, not to be influenced by the proceedings of the other; and the quoting them might beget reflections leading to a misunderstanding between the two Houses. 8 *Grey* 22.

Neither House can exercise any authority over a member or officer of the other, but should complain to the House of which he is, and leave the punishment to them. Where the complaint is of words disrespectfully spoken by a member of another House, it is difficult to obtain punishment, because of the rules supposed necessary to be observed (as to the immediate noting down of words) for the security of members. Therefore it is the duty of the House, and more particularly of the Speaker, to interfere immediately, and not to permit expressions to go unnoticed which may give a ground of complaint to the other House, and introduce proceedings and mutual accusations between the two Houses, which can hardly be terminated without difficulty and disorder. 3 *Hats.* 51.

No member may be present when a bill or any business concerning himself is debating, nor is any member to speak to the merits of it till he withdraws. 2 *Hats.* 219. The rule is, that if a charge against a member arise out of a report of a committee, or examination of witnesses in the House, as the member knows from that to what points he is to direct his exculpation, he may be heard to those points, before any question is moved or stated against him. He is then to be heard, and withdraw before any question is moved. But if the question itself is the charge, as for breach of order, or matter arising in the debate, there the charge must be stated, that is, the question must be moved, himself heard, and then to withdraw. 2 *Hats.* 121, 122.

Where the private interests of a member are concerned in a bill or question, he is to withdraw. And where such an interest has appeared, his voice has been disallowed, even after a division. In a case so contrary not only to the laws of decency, but to the fundamental principle of the social compact, which denies to any man to be a judge in his own cause, it is for the honor of the House that this rule, of immemorial observance, should be strictly adhered to. 2 *Hats.* 119, 121. 6 *Grey* 368.

No member is to come into the House with his head covered, nor to remove from one place to another with his hat on, nor is to put on his hat in coming in, or removing, until he be set down in his place. *Scob.* 6.

A question of order may be adjourned to give time to look into precedents. 2 *Hats.* 118.

In the Senate of the United States, every question of order is to be decided by the President, without debate: but if there be a doubt in his mind, he may call for the sense of the Senate. Rule 16.

In Parliament, all decisions of the Speaker may be controuled by the House. 3 *Grey* 319.

SEC. XVIII. ORDERS OF THE HOUSE.

OF right, the door of the House ought not to be shut, but to be kept by porters, or serjeants at arms, assigned for that purpose. *Mod. Ten. Parl.* 23.

By the rules of the Senate, on motion made and seconded, to shut the doors of the Senate on the discussion of any business which may in the opinion of a member require secrecy, the President shall direct the gallery to be cleared, and during the discussion of such motion, the doors shall remain shut. Rule 28.

No motion shall be deemed in order, to admit any person or persons whatever, within the doors of the Senate Chamber, to present any petition, memorial, or address, or to hear any such read. Rule 29.

The only case where a member has a right to insist on any thing is, where he calls for the execution of a subsisting order of the House. Here, there having been already a resolution, any member has a right to insist that the Speaker, or any other whose duty it is, shall carry it into execution; and no debate or delay can be had on it. Thus any member has a right to have the House or gallery cleared of strangers, an order existing for that purpose; or to have the House told when there is not a quorum present. 2 *Hats.* 87, 129. How far an order of the House is binding, see *Hakew.* 392.

But where an order is made that any particular matter be taken up on a particular day, there a question is to be put when it is called for, whether the House will now proceed to that matter? Where orders of the day are on important or interesting matter, they ought not to be proceeded on till an hour at which the House is usually full, *(which in Senate is at noon.)*

Orders of the day may be discharged at any time, and a new one made for a different day. 3 *Grey* 48, 313.[13]

When a session is drawing to a close, and the important bills are all brought in; the House, in order to prevent interruption by further unimportant bills, sometimes come to a resolution that no new bill be brought in, except it be sent from the other House. 3 *Grey* 156.

All orders of the House determine with the session; and one taken under such an order may, after the session is ended, be discharged on a habeas corpus. *Raym.* 120. *Jacob's L. D. by Ruffhead. Parliament,* 1 *Lev.* 165. *Prichard's case.*

Where the constitution authorises each House to determine the rules of its proceedings, it must mean in those cases legislative, executive or judiciary, submitted to them by the constitution, or in something relating to these, and necessary towards their execution. But orders and resolutions are sometimes entered in the journals, having no relation to these, such as acceptances of invitations to attend orations, to take part in processions, &c. These must be understood to be merely conventional among those who are willing to participate in the ceremony, and are therefore, perhaps, improperly placed among the records of the House.

13 This paragraph is italicized in Howell, *Parliamentary Writings*, but not in Smith's 1801 or Milligan's 1812 editions. The subject is not exclusive to the Senate, and Howell does not justify its italicization. Therefore, it is not italicized here.

SEC. XIX. PETITIONS.

A PETITION prays something. A remonstrance has no prayer. 1 *Grey* 58.

Petitions must be subscribed by the petitioners, *Scob.* 87. *L. Parl. c.* 22. 9 *Grey* 362. unless they are attending, 1 *Grey* 401. or unable to sign, and averred by a member. 3 *Grey* 418. But a petition not subscribed, but which the member presenting it affirmed to be all in the hand writing of the petitioner, and his name written in the beginning, was on the question (Mar. 14, 1800) received by the Senate. The averment of a member, or of somebody without doors, that they know the hand writing of the petitioners is necessary if it be questioned. 6 *Grey* 36. It must be presented by a member, not by the petitioners, and must be opened by him, holding it in his hand. 10 *Grey* 57.

Before any petition or memorial addressed to the Senate, shall be received and read at the table, whether the same shall be introduced by the President or a member, a brief statement of the contents of the petition or memorial shall verbally be made by the introducer. Rule 21.

Regularly a motion for receiving it must be made and seconded, and a question put whether it shall be received? But a cry from the House of "received," or even its silence, dispenses with the formality of this question. It is then to be read at the table and disposed of.

Sec. XX. MOTIONS.

WHEN a motion has been made, it is not to be put to the question or debated until it is seconded. *Scob.* 21.

The Senate say no motion shall be debated until the same shall be seconded. Rule 6.

It is then and not till then in possession of the House, and cannot be withdrawn but by leave of the House. It is to be put into writing, if the House or Speaker require it, and must be read to the House by the Speaker as often as any member desires it for his information. 2 *Hats.* 82.

The rule of the Senate is, when a motion shall be made and seconded, it shall be reduced to writing, if desired by the President, or any member, delivered in at the table, and read by the President before the same shall be debated. Rule 7.

It might be asked whether a motion for adjournment or for the orders of the day can be made by one member while another is speaking? It cannot. When two members offer to speak, he who rose first is to be heard, and it is a breach of order in another to interrupt him, unless by calling him to order, if he departs from it. And the question of order being decided, he is still to be heard through. A call for adjournment, or for the order of the day, or for the question, by gentlemen from their seats, is not a motion. No motion can be made without rising and addressing the chair. Such calls are themselves breaches of order, which though the member who has risen may respect, as an expression of the impatience of the House against further debate, yet, if he chuses, he has a right to go on.

SEC. XXI. RESOLUTIONS.

WHEN the House commands, it is by an "order." But facts, principles, their own opinions, and purposes, are expressed in the form of Resolutions.

A Resolution, for an allowance of money to the clerks, being moved, it was objected to as not in order, and so ruled by the chair. But on an appeal to the Senate (i.e. a call for their sense by the President on account of doubt in his mind according to Rule 16.*) the decision was overruled.* Journ. Sen. June 1, 1796. *I presume the doubt was, whether an allowance of money could be made otherwise than by bill.*

SEC. XXII. BILLS.

EVERY bill shall receive three readings, previous to its being passed; and the President shall give notice at each whether it be the first, second, or third; which readings shall be on three different days, unless the Senate unanimously direct otherwise, ***or, unless by a joint vote of both Houses, or the expiration of their term, the session is to be closed within three days.*** **Rule 13.**[14]

SEC. XXIII. BILLS, LEAVE TO BRING IN.

ONE day's notice at least shall be given of an intended motion for leave to bring in a bill. Rule 12.

14 In the Library copy and the Brooke copy, Jefferson underlined "which readings . . . otherwise" and added the annotation, "These words should be in Italics." This change is reflected in Milligan's 1812 edition. In the Library copy, "or unless . . . Rule 13" is an annotation by Jefferson at the end of Sec. 22, Para. 1, which is printed in Milligan's 1812 edition. See Howell, *Parliamentary Writings*, 429–30.

When a member desires to bring in a bill on any subject, he states to the House in general terms the causes for doing it, and concludes by moving for leave to bring in a bill intituled, &c. Leave being given, on the question, a committee is appointed to prepare and bring in the bill. The mover and seconder are always appointed of this committee, and one or more in addition. *Hakew.* 132. *Scob.* 40.

It is to be presented fairly written, without any erasure or interlineation, or the Speaker may refuse it. *Scob.* 41. 1 *Grey* 82, 84.

Sec. XXIV. BILLS, FIRST READING.

WHEN a bill is first presented, the clerk reads it at the table, and hands it to the Speaker, who rising, states to the House the title of the bill, that this is the first time of reading it, and the question will be whether it shall be read a second time? Then sitting down to give an opening for objections, if none be made, he rises again and puts the question whether it shall be read a second time? *Hakew.* 137, 141. A bill cannot be amended at the first reading. 6 *Grey* 286. nor is it usual for it to be opposed then: but it may be done and rejected. *D'Ewes* 335, *col.* 1. 3 *Hats.* 198.

Sec. XXV. BILLS, SECOND READING.

THE second reading must regularly be on another day. *Hakew.* 143. It is done by the clerk at the table, who then hands it to the Speaker. The Speaker, rising, states to the House the title of the bill, that this is the second time of reading it, and that the question will be whether it shall be committed, or engrossed and read a third time? But if the bill came from the other House, as it always comes engrossed, he states that the question will be whether it shall be read a third time? and before he has so reported the state of the bill, no one is to speak to it. *Hakew.* 143, 146.

In the Senate of the United States, the President reports the title of the bill, that this is the second time of reading it, that it is now to be considered as in a Committee of the Whole, and the question will be, whether it shall be read a third time? or, that it may be referred to a special committee.

Sec. XXVI. BILLS, COMMITMENT.

IF on motion and question it be decided that the bill shall be committed, it may then be moved to be referred to a committee of the whole House, or to a special committee. If the latter, the Speaker proceeds to name the committee. Any member also may name a single person, and the clerk is to write him down as of the committee. But the House have a controuling power over the names and number, if a question be moved against any one, and may in any case put in and put out whom they please.[15]

Those who take exceptions to some particulars in the bill are to be of the committee. But none who speak directly against the body of the bill. For he that would totally destroy, will not

15 In the Library copy, "4. Hats. 19." is an annotation by Jefferson at the end of Sec. 26, Para. 1, which does not appear in Milligan's 1812 edition.

amend it. *Hakew.* 146. *Town. coll.* 208. *D'Ewes.* 634. *col.* 2 *Scob* 47. or as is said, 5 *Grey* 145. the child is not to be put to a nurse that cares not for it. 6 *Grey* 373. It is therefore a constant rule "that no man is to be employed in any matter who has declared himself against it." And when any member who is against the bill hears himself named of its committee, he ought to ask to be excused. Thus March 7, 1606, Mr. Hadley was, on the question's being put, excused from being of a committee, declaring himself to be against the matter itself. *Scob.* 46.

No bill shall be committed or amended until it shall have been twice read, after which it may be referred to a committee. Rule 14.

All committees shall be appointed by ballot, and a plurality of voices shall make a choice. Rule 15.

The clerk may deliver the bill to any member of the committee. *Town. col.* 138. But it is usual to deliver it to him who is first named.

In some cases, the House has ordered a committee to withdraw immediately into the committee chamber, and act on, and bring back the bill, sitting the House. *Scob.* 48.

A committee meets when, and where they please, if the House has not ordered time and place for them. 6 *Grey* 370. But they can only act when together, and not by separate consultation and consent; nothing being the report of the committee but what has been agreed to in committee actually assembled.

A majority of the committee constitutes a quorum for business. *Elsynge's Method of passing Bills.* 11.

Any member of the House may be present at any select committee, but cannot vote, and must give place to all of the committee, and sit below them. *Elsynge* 12. *Scob.* 49.

But in 1626, April 24, the House of Commons resolved, that though any members may be present at the examination of witnesses, they may not be at the debate, disposition or penning of the business by the select committee. 4 *Hats.* 124.[16]

The committee have full power over the bill, or other paper committed to them, except that they cannot change the title or subject. 8 *Grey* 228.

The paper before a committee, whether select, or of the whole, may be a bill, resolutions, draught of an address, &c. and it may either originate with them, or be referred to them. In every case, the whole paper is read first by the clerk, and then by the chairman, by paragraphs, *Scob.* 49. pausing at the end of each paragraph, and putting questions for amending, if proposed. In the case of resolutions on distinct subjects, originating with themselves, a question is put on each separately, as amended, or unamended, and no final question on the whole: 3 *Hats.* 276. but if they relate to the same subject, a question is put on the whole. If it be a bill, draught of an address, or other paper originating with them, they proceed by paragraphs, putting questions for amending, either by insertion or striking out, if proposed: but no question on agreeing to the paragraphs separately. This is reserved to the close, when a question is put on the whole, for agreeing to it as amended, or unamended. But if it be a paper referred to them, they proceed to put questions of amendment, if proposed, but no final question on the whole: because all parts of the paper having been adopted by the House, stand

16 "But in 1626, April... 4 *Hats.* 124" is an annotation by Jefferson at the end of Sec. 26, Para. 9 in the Library copy and the Holmes copy and is printed in Milligan's 1812 edition. In the Holmes copy, Jefferson erroneously writes 1626 as 1606.

of course, unless altered, or struck out by a vote. Even if they are opposed to the whole paper, and think it cannot be made good by amendments, they cannot reject it, but must report it back to the House without amendments, and there make their opposition.

The natural order in considering and amending any paper is, to begin at the beginning, and proceed through it by paragraphs; and this order is so strictly adhered to in Parliament, that when a latter part has been amended, you cannot recur back and make any alteration in a former part. 2 *Hats.* 90. In numerous assemblies this restraint is doubtless important. *But in Senate of the United States, though in the main we consider and amend the paragraphs in their natural order, yet recurrences are indulged: and they seem on the whole, in that small body, to produce advantages overweighing their inconveniences.*

To this natural order of beginning at the beginning, there is a single exception found in Parliamentary usage. When a bill is taken up in committee, or on its second reading, they postpone the preamble, till the other parts of the bill are gone through. The reason is, that on consideration of the body of the bill, such alterations may therein be made as may also occasion the alteration of the preamble. *Scob.* 50. 7 *Grey* 431.

On this head the following case occurred in Senate, March 6, 1800. A resolution, which had no preamble, having been already amended by the House, so that a few words only of the original remained in it, a motion was made to prefix a preamble, which having an aspect very different from the resolution, the mover intimated that he should afterwards propose a correspondent amendment in the body of the resolution. It was objected that a preamble could not be taken up till the body of the resolution is done with. But the preamble was received: because we are in fact through the body of the resolution, we have amended that as far as amendments have been offered, and indeed till little of the original is left. It is the proper time, therefore, to consider a preamble: and whether the one offered be consistent with the resolution, is for the House to determine. The mover indeed, has intimated, that he shall offer a subsequent proposition for the body of the resolution; but the House is not in possession of it; it remains in his breast, and may be withheld. The rules of the House can only operate on what is before them. *The practice of the Senate too, allows recurrences backwards and forwards, for the purposes of amendment, not permitting amendments in a subsequent, to preclude those in a prior part, or e converso.*

When the committee is through the whole, a member moves that the committee may rise, and the chairman report the paper to the House, with, or without amendments, as the case may be. 2 *Hats.* 289, 292. *Scob.* 53. 2 *Hats.* 290. 8 *Scob.* 50.

When a vote is once passed in a committee, it cannot be altered but by the House, their votes being binding on themselves. 1607, *June* 4.

The committee may not erase, interline, or blot the bill itself; but must in a paper by itself, set down the amendments, stating the words which are to be inserted or omitted; *Scob.* 50. and where, by references to the page, line and word of the bill. *Scob.* 50.

Sec. XXVII. REPORT OF COMMITTEE.

THE chairman of the committee, standing in his place, informs the House, that the committee, to whom was referred such a bill, have, according to order, had the same under consideration, and have directed him to report the same without any amendment, or with sundry amendments, (as the case may be,) which he is ready to do, when the House pleases to receive it. And he, or any other, may move that it be now received. But the cry of "now, now," from the House, generally dispenses with the formality of a motion and question. He then reads the amendments with the coherence in the bill, and opens the alterations, and the reasons of the committee for such amendments, until he has gone through the whole. He then delivers it at the clerk's table, where the amendments reported are read by the clerk, without the coherence, whereupon the papers lie on the table, till the House at its convenience, shall take up the report. *Scob.* 52. *Hakew.* 148.

The report being made, the committee is dissolved, and can act no more without a new power. *Scob.* 51. But it may be revived by a vote, and the same matter recommitted to them. 4 *Grey* 361.

Sec. XXVIII. BILL, RECOMMITMENT.

AFTER a bill has been committed and reported, it ought not, in an ordinary course, to be recommitted. But in cases of importance, and for special reasons, it is sometimes recommitted, and usually to the same committee. *Hakew.* 151. If a report be recommitted before agreed to in the House, what has passed in committee is of no validity; the whole question is again before the committee, and a new resolution must be again moved, as if nothing had passed. 3 *Hats.* 131. *note.*

In Senate, January 1800, the salvage bill was recommitted three times after the commitment.

A particular clause of a bill may be committed without the whole bill; 3 *Hats.* 131. or so much of a paper to one, and so much to another committee.

SEC. XXIX. BILL, REPORT TAKEN UP.

WHEN the report of a paper originating with a committee, is taken up by the House, they proceed exactly as in committee. Here, as in committee, when the paragraphs have, on distinct questions, been agreed to seriatim, 5 *Grey* 366. 6 *Grey* 368. 8 *Grey* 47, 104, 360. 1 *Torbuck's Deb.* 125. 3 *Hats.* 348. no question needs be put on the whole report. 5 *Grey* 381.

On taking up a bill reported with amendments, the amendments only are read by the clerk. The Speaker then reads the first, and puts it to the question, and so on, till the whole are adopted or rejected, before any other amendment be admitted, except it be an amendment to an amendment. *Elsynge's Mem.* 53. When through the amendments of the committee, the Speaker pauses, and gives time for amendments to be proposed in the House to the body of the bill: as he does also if it has been reported without amendments; putting no questions but on amendments proposed: and when through the whole, he puts the question whether the bill shall be read a third time?

Sec. XXX. QUASI-COMMITTEE.

IF on the motion and question, the bill be not committed, or if no proposition for commitment be made, then the proceedings in the Senate of the United States, and in Parliament, are totally different. The former shall be first stated.

The 20th rule of the Senate says, "All bills, on a second reading, shall first be considered by the Senate in the same manner as if the Senate were in a committee of the whole, before they shall be taken up and proceeded on by the Senate agreeably to the standing rules, unless otherwise ordered:" that is to say, unless ordered to be referred to a special committee.

The proceeding of the Senate as in a committee of the whole, or in quasi-committee, is precisely as in a real committee of the whole, taking no questions but on amendments. When through the whole, they consider the quasi-committee as risen, the House resumed, without any motion, question, or resolution to that effect, and the President reports that "the House acting as in a committee of the whole, have had under their consideration the bill intituled, &c. and have made sundry amendments, which he will now report to the House." The bill is then before them as it would have been if reported from a committee, and questions are regularly to be put again on every amendment: which being gone through, the President pauses to give time to the House to propose amendments to the body of the bill, and when through, puts the question whether it shall be read a third time?

After progress in amending a bill in quasi-committee, a motion may be made to refer it to a special committee. If the motion prevails, it is equivalent in effect to the several votes that the committee rise, the House resume itself, discharge the committee of the whole, and refer the bill to a special committee. In that case the amendments already made fall. But if the motion fails, the quasi-committee stands in statu quo.

How far does this 20th rule subject the House when in quasi-committee, to the laws which regulate the proceedings of committees of the whole?

The particulars in which these differ from proceedings in the House, are the following.

1. In a committee, every member may speak as often as he pleases. 2. The votes of a committee may be rejected or altered when reported to the House. 3. A committee, even of the whole, cannot refer any matter to another committee. 4. In a committee, no previous question can be taken. The only means to avoid an improper discussion is, to move that the committee rise: and if it be apprehended that the same discussion will be attempted on returning into committee, the House can discharge them, and proceed itself on the business, keeping down the improper discussion by the previous question. 5. A committee cannot punish a breach of order, in the House, or in the gallery. 9 *Grey* 113. It can only rise and report it to the House, who may proceed to punish.

The 1st and 2d of these peculiarities attach to the quasi-committee of the Senate, as every day's practice proves; and seem to be the only ones to which the 20th rule meant to subject them. For it continues to be a House, and therefore, though it acts in some respects as a committee, in others it preserves its character as a House. Thus 3. It is in the daily habit of referring its business to a special committee. 4. It admits the previous question. If it did not, it would have no means of preventing an improper discussion;

not being able as a committee is, to avoid it by returning into the House: for the moment it would resume the same subject there, the 20th rule declares it again a quasi-committee. 5. It would doubtless exercise its powers as a House on any breach of order. 6. It takes a question by yea and nay, as the House does. 7. It receives messages from the President and the other House. 8. In the midst of a debate it receives a motion to adjourn, and adjourns as a House, not as a committee.

SEC. XXXI.
BILL, SECOND READING IN THE HOUSE.

IN Parliament, after the bill has been read a second time, if, on the motion and question, it be not committed, or if no proposition for commitment be made, the Speaker reads it by paragraphs, pausing between each, but putting no question but on amendments proposed; and when through the whole, he puts the question whether it shall be read a third time? if it came from the other House; or, if originating with themselves, whether it shall be engrossed and read a third time? The Speaker reads sitting, but rises to put questions. The clerk stands while he reads.

But the Senate of the United States is so much in the habit of making many and material amendments at the third reading, that it has become the practice not to engross a bill till it has passed. An irregular and dangerous practice; because, in this way, the paper which passes the Senate is not that which goes to the other House; and that which goes to the other House as the act of the Senate, has never been seen in Senate. In reducing numerous, difficult, and illegible amendments into the text, the Secretary may, with the most innocent intentions, commit errors, which can never again be corrected.

The bill being now as perfect as its friends can make it, this is the proper stage for those fundamentally opposed, to make their first attack. All attempts at earlier periods are with disjointed efforts; because many who do not expect to be in favor of the bill ultimately, are willing to let it go on to its perfect state, to take time to examine it themselves, and to hear what can be said for it; knowing that, after all, they will have sufficient opportunities of giving it their veto. Its two last stages therefore are reserved for this, that is to say, on the question whether it shall be read a third time? And lastly, whether it shall pass? The first of these is usually the most interesting contest; because then the whole subject is new and engaging, and the minds of the members having not yet been declared by any trying vote, the issue is the more doubtful. In this stage, therefore, is the main trial of strength between its friends and opponents: and it behoves every one to make up his mind decisively for this question, or he loses the main battle; and accident and management may, and often do, prevent a successful rallying on the next and last question whether it shall pass?

When the bill is engrossed, the title is to be endorsed on the back, and not within the bill. *Hakew.* 250.

Sec. XXXII. READING PAPERS.

WHERE papers are laid before the House, or referred to a committee, every member has a right to have them once read at the table, before he can be compelled to vote on them. But it is a great, though common error, to suppose that he has a right, toties quoties, to have acts, journals, accounts, or papers on the table read independently of the will of the House. The delay and interruption which this might be made to produce, evince the impossibility of the existence of such a right. There is indeed so manifest a propriety of permitting every member to have as much information as possible on every question on which he is to vote, that when he desires the reading, if it be seen that it is really for information, and not for delay, the Speaker directs it to be read without putting a question, if no one objects. But if objected to, a question must be put. 2 *Hats.* 117, 118.

It is equally an error, to suppose that any member has a right, without a question put, to lay a book or paper on the table, and have it read, on suggesting that it contains matter infringing on the privileges of the House. *Ib.*

For the same reason, a member has not a right to read a paper in his place, if it be objected to, without leave of the House. But this rigour is never exercised, but where there is an intentional or gross abuse of the time and patience of the House.

A member has not a right even to read his own speech, committed to writing, without leave. This also is to prevent an abuse of time; and therefore is not refused, but where that is intended. 2 *Grey* 227.

A report of a committee of the Senate on a bill from the House of Representatives, being under consideration, on motion that the report of the committee of the House of Representatives on the same bill be read in Senate, it passed in the negative; February 28, 1793.

Formerly when papers were referred to a committee, they used to be first read: but of late, only the titles; unless a member insists they shall be read, and then nobody can oppose it. 2 *Hats.* 117.

Sec. XXXIII. PRIVILEGED QUESTIONS.

WHILE a question is before the Senate, no motion shall be received unless for an amendment, for the previous question, or for postponing the main question, or to commit it, or to adjourn. Rule 8.

It is no possession of a bill, unless it be delivered to the clerk to be read, or the Speaker reads the title. *Lex. Parl.* 274. *Elsynge Mem.* 95. *Ord. House of Commons* 64.

It is a general rule, that the question first moved and seconded, shall be first put. *Scob.* 28, 22. 2 *Hats.* 81. But this rule gives way to what may be called privileged questions; and the privileged questions are of different grades among themselves.

A motion to adjourn simply takes place of all others; for otherwise, the House might be kept sitting against its will, and indefinitely. Yet this motion cannot be received after another question is actually put, and while the House is engaged in voting.

Orders of the day take place of all other questions, except for adjournment. That is to say, the question which is the subject of an order, is made a privileged one pro hac voce. The order is a repeal of the general rule as to this special case. When any member moves therefore for the orders of the day to be read, no further debate is permitted on the question which was before the House; for if the debate might proceed, it might continue through the day, and defeat the order. This motion, to entitle it to precedence, must be for the orders generally, and not for any particular one; and if it be carried on the question, "Whether the House will now proceed to the orders of the day," they must be read and proceeded on in the course in which they stand. 2 *Hats.* 83. For priority of order gives priority of right, which cannot be taken away but by another special order.

After these, there are other privileged questions which will require considerable explanation.

It is proper that every Parliamentary assembly should have certain forms of question so adapted, as to enable them fitly to dispose of every proposition which can be made to them. Such are 1. The previous question. 2. To postpone indefinitely. 3. To adjourn a question to a definite day. 4. To lie on the table. 5. To commit. 6. To amend. The proper occasion for each of these questions should be understood.

1. When a proposition is moved, which it is useless or inexpedient now to express or discuss, the previous question has been introduced for suppressing for that time the motion and its discussion. 3 *Hats.* 188, 189.

2. But as the previous question gets rid of it only for that day, and the same proposition may recur the next day, if they wish to suppress it for the whole of that session, they postpone it indefinitely. 3 *Hats.* 183. This quashes the proposition for that session, as an indefinite adjournment is a dissolution, or the continuance of a suit sine die is a discontinuance of it.

3. When a motion is made which it will be proper to act on, but information is wanted, or something more pressing claims

the present time, the question or debate is adjourned to such day within the session as will answer the views of the House. 2 *Hats.* 81. And those who have spoken before may not speak again when the adjourned debate is resumed. 2 *Hats.* 73. Sometimes, however, this has been abusively used, by adjourning it to a day beyond the session, to get rid of it altogether, as would be done by an indefinite postponement.

4. When the House has something else which claims its present attention, but would be willing to reserve in their power to take up a proposition whenever it shall suit them, they order it to lie on their table. It may then be called for at any time.

5. If the proposition will want more amendment and digestion than the formalities of the House will conveniently admit, they refer it to a committee.

6. But if the proposition be well digested and may need but few and simple amendments, and especially if these be of leading consequence, they then proceed to consider and amend it themselves.

The Senate, in their practice, vary from this regular gradation of forms. Their practice, comparatively with that of Parliament stands thus:

For the Parliamentary,		The Senate uses,
Postpmt. indefinite	=	Postp. to a day beyond the session.
Adjournment	=	Postp. to a day within the session.
Lying on the Table	=	Postpmt. indefinite. Lying on the table.

In their 8th rule therefore, which declares that while a question is before the Senate, no motion shall be received unless it be for the previous question, or to postpone, commit, or amend the main question, the term postponement must be understood according to their broad use of it, and not in its Parliamentary sense. Their rule then establishes as privileged questions, the previous question, postponement, commitment and amendment.

But it may be asked, have these questions any privilege among themselves? Or, are they so equal, that the common principle of the "first moved, first put" takes place among them? This will need explanation. Their competitions may be as follow:

1. Prev. Qu. and	Postpone, Commit, Amend	In the 1st, 2d, and 3d classes and the 1st member of the 4th class, the rule "first moved first put" takes place.
2. Postpone and	Prev. Qu. Commit, Amend.	
3. Commit and	Prev. Qu. Postpone, Amend.	
4. Amend and	Prev. Qu. Postpone, Commit.	

In the first class, where the previous question is first moved, the effect is peculiar. For it not only prevents the after motion to postpone or commit from being put to question before it, but also, from being put after it. For if the previous question be decided affirmatively, to wit, that the main question shall now be put, it would of course be against the decision to postpone or commit. And if it be decided negatively, to wit, that the main question shall not now be put, this puts the House out of possession of the main question, and consequently there is nothing before them to postpone or commit. So that neither voting for, or against the previous question, will enable the advocates for postponing or committing to get at their object. Whether it may be amended, shall be examined hereafter.

2d Class. If postponement be decided affirmatively, the proposition is removed from before the House, and consequently there is no ground for the previous question, commitment, or amendment. But, if decided negatively, that it shall not be postponed, the main question may then be suppressed by the previous question, or may be committed, or amended.

The 3d class is subject to the same observations as the 2d.

The 4th class. Amendment of the main question first moved, and afterwards the previous question, the question of amendment shall be first put.

Amendment and postponement competing, postponement is first put, as the equivalent proposition to adjourn the main question would be in Parliament. The reason is, that the question for amendment is not suppressed by postponing or adjourning the main question, but remains before the House whenever the main question is resumed: and it might be that the occasion for other urgent business might go by, and be lost by length of debate on the amendment, if the House had it not in their power to postpone the whole subject.

Amendment and commitment. The question for committing, though last moved, shall be first put: because, in truth, it facilitates and befriends the motion to amend. *Scobell* is express. "On a motion to amend a bill, any one may notwithstanding, move to commit it, and the question for commitment shall be first put." *Scob.* 46.

We have hitherto considered the case of two or more of the privileged questions contending for privilege between themselves, when both were moved on the original or main question; but now let us suppose one of them to be moved, not on the original primary question, but on the secondary one: *e. g.*

Suppose a motion to postpone, commit or amend the main question, and that it be moved to suppress that motion by putting a previous question on it. This is not allowed: because it would embarrass questions too much to allow them to be piled on one another several stories high; and the same result may be had in a more simple way, by deciding against the postponement, commitment or amendment. 2 *Hats.* 81, 2, 3, 4.

Suppose a motion for the previous question, or commitment, or amendment of the main question, and that it be then moved to postpone the motion for the previous question, or for commitment, or amendment of the main question. 1. It would be absurd to postpone the previous question, commitment or amendment alone, and thus separate the appendage from its principal. Yet it must be postponed separately from its original, if at all: because the 8th rule of Senate says, that when a main question is before the House, no motion shall be received but to commit, amend, or pre-question the original question, which is the Parliamentary doctrine also. Therefore the motion to postpone the secondary motion for the previous question, or for committing or amending, cannot be received. 2. This is a piling of questions one on another, which, to avoid embarrassment, is not allowed. 3. The same result may be had more simply, by voting against the previous question, commitment or amendment.

Suppose a commitment moved of a motion for the previous question, or to postpone or amend. The 1st, 2d and 3d reasons before stated, all hold good against this.

Suppose an amendment moved to a motion for the previous question. Answer. The previous question cannot be amended. Parliamentary usage, as well as the 9th rule of the Senate has fixed its form to be "Shall the main question be now put?" *i. e.* at this instant. And as the present instant is but one, it can admit of no modification. To change it to to-morrow, or any other moment, is without example, and without utility. But suppose a motion to amend a motion for postponement; as to one day instead of another, or to a special, instead of indefinite time. The useful character of amendment, gives it a privilege of attaching itself to a secondary and privileged motion. That is, we may amend a postponement of a main question. So we may amend a commitment of a main question, as by adding, for example, "with instructions to enquire, &c." In like manner, if an amendment be moved to an amendment, it is admitted. But it would not be admitted in another degree: to wit, to amend an amendment to an amendment, of a main question. This would lead to too much embarrassment. The line must be drawn somewhere, and usage has drawn it after the amendment to the amendment. The same result must be sought by deciding against the amendment to the amendment, and then moving it again as it was wished to be amended. In this form it becomes only an amendment to an amendment.

In filling a blank with a sum, the largest sum shall be first put to the question by the 18*th rule of the Senate*, contrary to the rule of Parliament which privileges the smallest sum and longest time.

5 *Grey* 179. 2 *Hats.* 81, 83. 3 *Hats.* 132, 133. And this is considered to be not in the form of an amendment to the question; but as alternative, or successive originals. In all cases of time or number, we must consider whether the larger comprehends the lesser, as in a question to what day a postponement shall be, the number of a committee, amount of a fine, term of an imprisonment, term of irredeemability of a loan, or the terminus in quem, in any other case. Then the question must begin a maximo. Or whether the lesser concludes the greater, as in questions on the limitation of the rate of interest, on what day the session shall be closed by adjournment, on what day the next shall commence, when an act shall commence, or the terminus a quo in any other case, where the question must begin a minimo. The object being not to begin at that extreme, which, and more, being within every man's wish, no one could negative it, and yet, if he should vote in the affirmative, every question for more would be precluded: but at that extreme which would unite few, and then to advance or recede, till you get to a number which will unite a bare majority. 3 *Grey* 376, 384, 385. "The fair question in this case is not that to which and more all will agree, but whether there shall be addition to the question." 1 *Grey* 365.

Another exception to the rule of priority is, when a motion has been made to strike out, or agree to a paragraph. Motions to amend it are to be put to the question before a vote is taken on striking out, or agreeing to the whole paragraph.

But there are several questions, which being incidental to every one, will take place of every one, privileged or not; to wit, a question of order arising out of any other question, must be decided before that question. 2 *Hats.* 88.

A matter of privilege arising out of any question, or from a quarrel between two members, or any other cause, supersedes the consideration of the original question, and must be first disposed of. 2 *Hats.* 88.

Reading papers relative to the question before the House. This question must be put before the principal one. 2 *Hats.* 88.

Leave asked to withdraw a motion. The rule of Parliament being, that a motion made and seconded is in possession of the House, and cannot be withdrawn without leave, the very terms of the rule imply that leave may be given, and consequently may be asked and put to the question.

SEC. XXXIV. THE PREVIOUS QUESTION.

WHEN any question is before the House, any member may move a previous question "Whether that question (called the main question) shall now be put?" If it pass in the affirmative, then the main question is to be put immediately, and no man may speak any thing further to it, either to add or alter. *Memor. in Hakew.* 28. 4 *Grey* 27.

The previous question being moved and seconded, the question from the chair shall be, "Shall the main question be now put?" and if the nays prevail, the main question shall not then be put. Rule 9.

This kind of question is understood by Mr. Hatsell to have been introduced in 1604. 2 *Hats.* 80. Sir Henry Vane introduced it. 2 *Grey* 113, 114. 3 *Grey* 384. When the question was put in this form, "Shall the main question be put?" a determination in the negative suppressed the main question during the session; but since the words "now put" are used, they exclude it for the present only. Formerly indeed, only till the present debate was over; 4 *Grey* 43. but now, for that day and no longer. 2 *Grey* 113, 114.

Before the question "whether the main question shall now be put?" any person might, formerly, have spoken to the main question, because otherwise he would be precluded from speaking to it at all. *Mem. in Hakew.* 28.

The proper occasion for the previous question is, when a subject is brought forward of a delicate nature, as to high personages, &c. or the discussion of which may call forth observations which might be of injurious consequences. Then the previous question is proposed: and, in the modern usage, the discussion of the main question is suspended, and the debate confined to the previous question. The use of it has been extended abusively to other cases: but in these it is an embarrassing procedure: its uses would be as well answered by other more simple Parliamentary forms, and therefore it should not be favoured, but restricted within as narrow limits as possible.

Whether a main question may be amended after the previous question on it has been moved and seconded? 2 *Hats.* 88. says, If the previous question has been moved and seconded, and also proposed from the chair, (by which he means stated by the Speaker for debate) it has been doubted whether an amendment can be admitted to the main question. He thinks it may, after the previous question moved and seconded; but not after it has been proposed from the chair. In this case he thinks the friends to the amendment must vote that the main question be not now put; and then move their amended question, which being made new by the amendment, is no longer the same which has been just suppressed, and therefore may be proposed as a new one.

But this proceeding certainly endangers the main question, by dividing its friends, some of whom may chuse it unamended, rather than lose it altogether: while others of them may vote, as Hatsell advises, that the main question be not now put, with a view to move it again in an amended form. The enemies to the main question, by this manœuvre of the previous question, get the enemies to the amendment added to them on the first vote, and throw the friends of the main question under the embarrassment of rallying again as they can. To support his opinion too, he makes the deciding circumstance, whether an amendment may or may not be made, to be that the previous question has been proposed from the chair. But as the rule is that the House is in possession of a question as soon as it is moved and seconded, it cannot be more than possessed of it by its being also proposed from the chair. It may be said indeed, that the object of the previous question being to get rid of a question, which it is not expedient should be discussed, this object may be defeated by moving to amend, and, in the discussion of that motion, involving the subject of the main question. But so may the object of the previous question be defeated by moving the amended question, as Mr. Hatsell proposes, after the decision against putting the original question. He acknowledges too, that the practice has been to admit previous amendment, and only cites a few late instances to the contrary. On the whole, I should think it best to decide it ab inconvenienti, to wit, which is most inconvenient, to put it in the power of one side of the House to defeat a proposition by hastily moving the previous question, and thus forcing the main question to be put unamended; or to put in the power of the other side to force on, incidentally at least, a discussion which would be better avoided? Perhaps the last is the least inconvenience; in as much as the Speaker, by confining the discussion rigorously to the amendment only, may prevent their going into the main question, and inasmuch also as so great a proportion of the cases in which the previous question is called for, are fair and proper subjects of public discussion, and ought not to be obstructed by a formality introduced for questions of a peculiar character.

Sec. XXXV. AMENDMENTS.

ON an amendment being moved, a member who has spoken to the main question may speak again to the amendment. *Scob.* 23.

If an amendment be proposed, inconsistent with one already agreed to, it is a fit ground for its rejection by the House; but not within the competence of the Speaker to suppress as if it were against order. For were he permitted to draw questions of consistence within the vortex of order, he might usurp a negative on important modifications, and suppress, instead of subserving, the legislative will.

Amendments may be made so as totally to alter the nature of the proposition; and it is a way of getting rid of a proposition, by making it bear a sense different from what was intended by the movers, so that they vote against it themselves. 2 *Hats.* 79, 4, 82, 84. A new bill may be ingrafted by way of amendment, on the words "Be it enacted, &c." 1 *Grey* 190, 192.

If it be proposed to amend by leaving out certain words, it may be moved as an amendment to this amendment, to leave out a part of the words of the amendment, which is equivalent to leaving them in the bill. 2 *Hats.* 80, 9. The Parliamentary question is always, whether the words shall stand part of the bill?

When it is proposed to amend by inserting a paragraph, or part of one, the friends of the paragraph may make it as perfect as they can by amendments, before the question is put for inserting it. If it be received, it cannot be amended afterwards, in the same stage; because the House, has on a vote, agreed to it in that form. In like manner, if it is proposed to amend by striking out a paragraph, the friends of the paragraph are first to make it as perfect as they can by amendments, before the question is put for striking it out. If, on the question, it be retained, it cannot be amended afterwards: because a vote against striking out, is equivalent to a vote agreeing to it in that form.

When it is moved to amend, by striking out certain words, and inserting others, the manner of stating the question is, first to read the whole passage to be amended as it stands at present, then the words proposed to be struck out, next those to be inserted, and lastly, the whole passage as it will be when amended. And the question, if desired, is then to be divided, and put first on striking out. If carried, it is next on inserting the words proposed. If that be lost, it may be moved to insert others, 2 *Hats.* 80, 7.

A motion is made to amend by striking out certain words, and inserting others in their place, which is negatived. Then it is moved to strikeout the same words, and to insert others, of a tenor entirely different from those first proposed. It is negatived.

Then it is moved to strike out the same words and insert nothing, which is agreed to. All this is admissible; because to strike out and insert A, is one proposition. To strike out and insert B, is a different proposition. And to strike out and insert nothing, is still different. And the rejection of one proposition does not preclude the offering a different one. Nor would it change the case were the first motion divided, by putting the question first on striking out, and that negatived. For as putting the whole motion to the question at once, would not have precluded, the putting the half of it cannot do it.*

But if it had been carried affirmatively to strike out the words, and to insert A, it could not afterwards be permitted to strike out A and insert B. The mover of B should have notified while the insertion of A was under debate, that he would move to insert B. In which case, those who preferred it, would join in rejecting A.

After A is inserted, however, it may be moved to strike out a portion of the original paragraph, comprehending A, provided the coherence to be struck out, be so substantial as to make this effectively a different proposition. For then it is resolved into the common case of striking out a paragraph after amending it. Nor does any thing forbid a new insertion, instead of A and its coherence.

* In the case of a division of the question, and a decision against striking out, I advance doubtingly the opinion here expressed. I find no authority either way; and I know it may be viewed under a different aspect. It may be thought that having decided separately not to strike out the passage, the same question for striking out cannot be put over again, though with a view to a different insertion. Still I think it more reasonable and convenient, to consider the striking out and insertion, as forming one proposition; but should readily yield to any evidence that the contrary is the practice in Parliament.

In Senate, January 25, 1798, a motion to postpone until the 2d Tuesday in February some amendments proposed to the constitution.... The words "until the 2d Tuesday in February," were struck out by way of amendment. Then it was moved, to add "until the 1st day of June." Objected that it was not in order, as the question should be first put on the longest time; therefore, after a shorter time decided against, a longer cannot be put to question. It was answered, that this rule takes place only in filling blanks for time. But when a specific time stands part of a motion, that may be struck out as well as any other part of the motion; and when struck out, a motion may be received to insert any other. In fact, it is not till they are struck out, and a blank for the time thereby produced, that the rule can begin to operate, by receiving all the propositions for different times, and putting the questions successively on the longest. Otherwise, it would be in the power of the mover, by inserting originally a short time, to preclude the possibility of a longer. For till the short time is struck out, you cannot insert a longer; and if, after it is struck out, you cannot do it, then it cannot be done at all. Suppose the first motion had been to amend by striking out "the 2d Tuesday of February," and inserting instead thereof "the 1st of June." It would have been regular then to divide the question, by proposing first the question to strike out, and then that to insert. Now this is precisely the effect of the present proceeding; only instead of one motion and two questions, there are two motions and two questions, to effect it; the motion being divided as well as the question.

When the matter contained in two bills might be better put into one, the manner is to reject the one, and incorporate its matter into another bill by way of amendment. **Or, both may**

be referred to a committee to be made into one bill. 4 *Hats.* 319.[17] So if the matter of one bill would be better distributed into two, any part may be struck out by way of amendment, and put into a new bill. If a section is to be transposed, a question must be put on striking it out where it stands, and another for inserting it in the place desired.

A bill passed by the one House with blanks. These may be filled up by the other, by way of amendments, returned to the first as such and passed. 3 *Hats.* 83.

The number prefixed to the section of a bill, being merely a marginal indication, and no part of the text of the bill, the clerk regulates that, the House or committee is only to amend the text.

Sec. XXXVI. DIVISION OF THE QUESTION.

IF a question contain more parts than one, it may be divided into two or more questions. *Mem. in Hakew.* 29. But not as the right of an individual member, but with the consent of the House. For who is to decide whether a question is complicated or not? where it is complicated? into how many propositions it may be divided? The fact is, that the only mode of separating a complicated question is, by moving amendments to it; and these must be decided by the House on a question, unless the House orders it to be divided: as on the question December 2, 1640, making void the election of the knights for Worcester, on a motion, it was resolved, to make two questions of it, to wit, one on each knight. 2 *Hats.* 85, 86. So wherever there are several names in a question, they may be divided and put one by one.

17 "Or, both may... 4 *Hats.* 319." is an annotation by Jefferson in Sec. 35, Para. 11 in the Library copy and the Holmes copy and is printed in Milligan's 1812 edition.

9 *Grey* 444. So 1729, April 17, on an objection that a question was complicated, it was separated by amendment. 2 *Hats.* 79, 5.

The soundness of these observations will be evident from the embarrassments produced by the 10th rule of the Senate, which says, "*if the question in debate contain several points, any member may have the same divided.*"[18]

1798, *May* 30, *the Alien Bill in quasi-committee. To a section and proviso in the original, had been added two new provisoes by way of amendment. On a motion to strike out the section as amended, the question was desired to be divided. To do this, it must be put first on striking out either the former proviso, or some distinct member of the section. But when nothing remains but the last member of the section, and the provisoes, they cannot be divided so as to put the last member to question by itself; for the provisoes might thus be left standing alone, as exceptions to a rule, when the rule is taken away; or the new provisoes might be left to a second question, after having been decided on once before at the same reading; which is contrary to rule. But the question must be on striking out the last member of the section as amended. This sweeps away the exceptions with the rule, and relieves from inconsistence. A question to be divisible, must comprehend points so distinct and entire, that one of them being taken away, the other may stand entire. But a proviso or exception, without an enacting clause, does not contain an entire point or proposition.*

18 The text starting at "if the question…" through the end of Sec. 36 is not italicized in Smith's 1801 edition, nor is there an annotation by Jefferson indicating it should be italicized. This may have been a decision by Milligan to italicize passages about the Senate, or perhaps Jefferson communicated this change to Milligan. For additional discussion of the origins of this text, see Howell, *Parliamentary Writings*, note 15, page 342.

May 31. *The same bill being before the Senate.... There was a proviso that the bill should not extend,* 1. *To any foreign minister; nor,* 2. *to any person to whom the President should give a passport; nor,* 3. *to any alien merchant conforming himself to such regulations as the President shall prescribe, and a division of the question into its simplest elements, was called for. It was divided into four parts, the* 4*th taking in the words "conforming himself, &c." It was objected that the words "any alien merchant," could not be separated from their modifying words "conforming, &c." because these words, if left by themselves, contain no substantive idea, will make no sense. But admitting that the divisions of a paragraph into separate questions must be so made as that each part may stand by itself, yet, the House having, on the question, retained the two first divisions, the words "any alien merchant" may be struck out, and their modifying words will then attach themselves to the preceding description of persons, and become a modification of that description.*

When a question is divided, after the question on the 1*st member, the* 2*d is open to debate and amendment: because it is a known rule, that a person may rise and speak at any time before the question has been completely decided, by putting the negative, as well as affirmative side. But the question is not completely put, when the vote has been taken on the first member only. One half of the question, both affirmative and negative, remains still to be put.* See Execut. Journ. June 25, 1795. *The same decision by President Adams.*

Sec. XXXVII. CO-EXISTING QUESTIONS.

IT may be asked, whether the House can be in possession of two motions or propositions at the same time? So that, one of them being decided, the other goes to question without being moved anew? The answer must be special. When a question is interrupted by a vote of adjournment, it is thereby removed from before the House, and does not stand ipso facto before them at their next meeting: but must come forward in the usual way. So, when it is interrupted by the order of the day. Such other privileged questions also as dispose of the main question (e. g. the previous question, postponement or commitment,) remove it from before the House. But it is only suspended by a motion to amend, to withdraw, to read papers, or, by a question of order or privilege, and stands again before the House when these are decided. None but the class of privileged questions can be brought forward, while there is another question before the House, the rule being that when a motion has been made and seconded, no other can be received, except it be a privileged one.

Sec. XXXVIII. EQUIVALENT QUESTIONS.

IF, on a question for rejection, a bill be retained, it passes of course to its next reading. *Hakew.* 141. *Scob.* 42. And a question for a second reading, determined negatively, is a rejection without farther question. 4 *Grey* 149. And see *Elsynge's Memor.* 42. in what cases questions are to be taken for rejection.

Where questions are perfectly equivalent, so that the negative of the one amounts to the affirmative of the other, and leaves no other alternative, the decision of the one concludes necessarily the other. 4 *Grey* 157. Thus the negative of striking out amounts to the affirmative of agreeing; and therefore, to put a question on agreeing after that on striking out, would be to put the same question in effect twice over. Not so in questions of amendments between the two Houses. A motion to recede being negatived, does not amount to a positive vote to insist, because there is another alternative, to wit, to adhere.

A bill originating in one House, is passed by the other with an amendment. A motion in the originating House to agree to the amendment is negatived. Does there result from this a vote of disagreement, or must the question on disagreement be expressly voted? The questions respecting amendments from another House are, 1. To agree. 2. Disagree. 3. Recede. 4. Insist. 5. Adhere.

<table>
<tr><td>1st. To agree.
2d. To disagree.</td><td colspan="2">Either of these concludes the other necessarily: for the positive of either is exactly the equivalent of the negative of the other, and no other alternative remains. On either motion amendments to the amendment may be proposed, e. g. if it be moved to disagree, those who are for the amendment have a right to propose amendments, and to make it as perfect as they can, before the question of disagreeing is put.</td></tr>
<tr><td>3d. To recede.</td><td>You may then either insist or adhere.</td><td rowspan="3">Consequently the negative of these is not equivalent to a positive vote the other way. It does not raise so necessary an implication as may authorise the secretary by inference to enter another vote: for two alternatives still remain, either of which may be adopted by the House.</td></tr>
<tr><td>4th. To insist.</td><td>You may then either recede or adhere.</td></tr>
<tr><td>5th. To adhere.</td><td>You may then either recede or insist.</td></tr>
</table>

SEC. XXXIX. THE QUESTION.

THE question is to be put first on the affirmative, and then on the negative side.

After the Speaker has put the affirmative part of the question, any member who has not spoken before to the question, may rise and speak before the negative be put. Because it is no full question till the negative part be put. *Scob.* 23. 2 *Hats.* 73.

But in small matters, and which are of course, such as receiving petitions, reports, withdrawing motions, reading papers, &c. the Speaker most commonly supposes the consent of the House, where no objection is expressed, and does not give them the trouble of putting the question formally. *Scob.* 22. 2 *Hats.* 79, 2, 87. 5 *Grey* 129. 9 *Grey* 301.

SEC. XL. BILLS, THIRD READING.

TO prevent bills from being passed by surprise, the House, by a standing order, directs that they shall not be put on their passage before a fixed hour, naming one at which the House is commonly full. *Hakew.* 153.

The usage of the Senate is not to put bills on their passage till noon.

A bill reported and passed to the third reading cannot on that day be read the third time and passed. Because this would be to pass on two readings in the same day.

At the third reading, the clerk reads the bill and delivers it to the Speaker, who states the title, that it is the third time of reading the bill, and that the question will be whether it shall pass? Formerly, the Speaker, or those who prepared a bill, prepared also a breviate or summary statement of its contents, which the Speaker read when he declared the state of the bill, at the several readings. Sometimes however, he read the bill itself, especially on its passage. *Hakew.* 136, 137, 153. *Coke* 22, 115. Latterly, instead of this, he, at the third reading, states the whole contents of the bill verbatim, only instead of reading the formal parts, "Be it enacted, &c." he states that "the preamble recites so and so. . . . the 1st section enacts that, &c. the 2d section enacts, &c."

But in the Senate of the United States, both of these formalities are dispensed with; the breviate presenting but an imperfect view of the bill, and being capable of being made to present a false one: and the full statement being an useless waste of time, immediately after a full reading by the clerk; and especially as every member has a printed copy in his hand.

A bill on the third reading, is not to be committed for the matter or body thereof; but to receive some particular clause or proviso, it hath been sometimes suffered, but as a thing very unusual. *Hakew.* 156. thus 27 *El.* 1584. a bill was committed on the third reading, having been formerly committed on the second, but is declared not usual. *D'Ewes* 337. *col.* 2, 414, *col.* 2.

When an essential provision has been omitted, rather than erase the bill, and render it suspicious, they add a clause on a separate paper, engrossed and called a ryder, which is read and put to the question three times.[19] *Elsynge's Memorials* 59. 6 *Grey* 335. 1 *Blackst.* 183. For examples of ryders see 3 *Hats.* 121, 122, 124, 126. Every one is at liberty to bring in a ryder without asking leave. 10 *Grey* 52.

19 Howell, *Parliamentary Writings*, italicizes this sentence, but it is not italicized in Smith's 1801 or Milligan's 1812 editions, there is no annotation by Jefferson on this text, nor does it appear to be peculiar to the Senate.

It is laid down as a general rule, that amendments proposed at the second reading shall be twice read, and those proposed at the third reading thrice read; as also all amendments from the other House. *Town. col.* 19, 23, 24, 25, 26, 27, 28.

It is with great, and almost invincible reluctance, that amendments are admitted at this reading, which occasion erasures or interlineations. Sometimes a proviso has been cut off from a bill; sometimes erased. 9 *Grey* 513.

This is the proper stage for filling up blanks; for if filled up before, and now altered by erasure, it would be peculiarly unsafe.

At this reading the bill is debated afresh, and for the most part is more spoken to, at this time, than on any of the former readings. *Hakew.* 153.

The debate on the question whether it should be read a third time? has discovered to its friends and opponents the arguments on which each side relies, and which of these appear to have influence with the House; they have had time to meet them with new arguments, and to put their old ones into new shapes. The former vote has tried the strength of the first opinion and furnished grounds to estimate the issue; and the question now offered for its passage, is the last occasion which is ever to be offered for carrying or rejecting it.

When the debate is ended, the Speaker, holding the bill in his hand, puts the question for its passage, by saying, "Gentlemen, all you who are of opinion that this bill shall pass, say aye," and after the answer of the ayes, "All those of the contrary opinion say no." *Hakew.* 154.

After the bill is passed, there can be no further alteration of it in any point. *Hakew.* 159.

Sec. XLI. DIVISION OF THE HOUSE.

THE affirmative and negative of the question having been both put and answered, the Speaker declares whether the yeas or nays have it by the sound, if he be himself satisfied, and it stands as the judgment of the House. But if he be not himself satisfied which voice is the greater, or if, before any other member comes into the House, or before any new motion made (for it is too late after that) any member shall rise and declare himself dissatisfied with the Speaker's decision, then the Speaker is to divide the House. *Scob.* 24. 2 *Hats.* 140.

When the House of Commons is divided, the one party goes forth, and the other remains in the House. This has made it important which go forth, and which remain; because the latter gain all the indolent, the indifferent and inattentive. Their general rule therefore is, that those who give their votes for the preservation of the orders of the House, shall stay in, and those who are for introducing any new matter or alteration, or proceeding contrary to the established course, are to go out. But this rule is subject to many exceptions and modifications. 2 *Hats.* 134. 1 *Rush. p.* 3, *fol.* 92. *Scob.* 43, 52. *Co.* 12, 116. *D'Ewes.* 505. *col.* 1. *Mem. in Hakew.* 25, 29. as will appear by the following statement of who go forth.

The one party being gone forth, the Speaker names two tellers from the affirmative, and two from the negative side, who first count those sitting in the House, and report the number to the Speaker. Then they place themselves within the door, two on each side, and count those who went forth, as they come in, and report the number to the Speaker. *Mem. in Hakew.* 26.

Petition that it be received,*	Ayes.	
Read.		
Lie on the table,	Noes.	
Rejected after refusal to lie on table,		
Referred to a committee, or farther proceeding,	Ayes.	
Bill, that it be brought in,		
Read 1st or 2d time,		
Engrossed, or read 3d time,	Ayes.	
Proceeding on every other stage,		
Committed,		
To committee of the whole,	Noes.	
To a select committee,	Ayes.	
Report of bill to lie on table,	Noes.	
Be *now* read,	Ayes.	
Be taken into consideration 3 months hence,	30 P. J.	251.
Amendments be read a 2d time,	Noes.	
Clause offered on report of bill be read 2d time,		
For receiving a clause,	Ayes.	334.
With amendments be engrossed,		395.
That a bill be *now* read a 3d time,	Noes.	398.
Receive a ryder,		260.
Pass,	Ayes.	259.
Be printed,		
Committees. That A take the chair,		
To agree to the whole or any part of report,		
That the H. do *now* resolve into committee,		291.
Speaker. That he now leave the chair, after order to go into committee,	Noes.	
That he issue warrant for a new writ,		
Member. That none be absent without leave,		
Witness. That he be further examined,	Ayes.	344.
Previous question,	Noes.	

*Noes 9 Grey 365.

Question	Who go forth
Blanks. That they be filled with the largest sum, Amendments. That words stand part of	Ayes.
Lords. That their amendment be read a 2d time,	Noes.
Messenger be received, Orders of day to be now read, if before 2 o'clock,	Ayes.
If after 2 o'clock,	Noes.
Adjournment, till the next sitting day, if before 4 o'clock,	Ayes.
if after 4 o'clock,	Noes.
Over a sitting day (unless a previous resolution,)	Ayes.
Over the 30th of January,	Noes.
For sitting on Sunday or any other day, not being a sitting day,	Ayes.

A mistake in the report of the tellers may be rectified after the report made. 2 *Hats.* 145. *note.*

But in both Houses of Congress, all these intricacies are avoided. The Ayes first rise and are counted, standing in their places, by the President or Speaker. Then they sit, and the Noes rise and are counted in like manner.

In Senate, if they be equally divided, the Vice-President announces his opinion, which decides.

The constitution however has directed that "the Yeas and Nays of the members of either House on any question shall, at the desire of one fifth of those present, be entered on the journal." And again, that in all cases of reconsidering a bill, disapproved by the President, and returned with his objections, "the votes of both Houses shall be determined by Yeas and Nays, and the names of the persons voting for and against the bill, shall be entered on the journals of each House respectively."

By the 11th rule of the Senate, when the Yeas and Nays shall be called for by one fifth of the members present, each member called upon, shall, unless for special reasons he be excused by the Senate, declare openly and without debate, his assent or dissent to the question. In taking the Yeas and Nays, and upon the call of the House, the names of the members shall be taken alphabetically.

When it is proposed to take the vote by Yeas and Nays, the President or Speaker states, that "the question is, whether e. g. the bill shall pass? that it is proposed that the Yeas and Nays shall be entered on the journal. Those therefore who desire it will rise." If he finds and declares that one fifth have risen, he then states that "those who are of opinion that the bill shall pass are to answer in the affirmative, those of the contrary opinion in the negative." The clerk then calls over the names alphabetically, notes the Yea or Nay of each, and gives the list to the President or Speaker, who declares the result. In Senate, if there be an equal division, the secretary calls on the Vice-President, and notes his affirmative or negative, which becomes the decision of the House.

In the House of Commons, every member must give his vote the one way or the other. *Scob.* 24. As it is not permitted to any one to withdraw who is in the House when the question is put, nor is any one to be told in the division who was not in when the question was put. 2 *Hats.* 140.

This last position is always true when the vote is by Yeas and Nays; where the negative as well as affirmative of the question is stated by the President at the same time, and the vote of both sides begins and proceeds pari passu. It is true also when the question is put in the usual way, if the negative has also been put.

But if it has not, the member entering, or any other member, may speak, and even propose amendments, by which the debate may be opened again, and the question be greatly deferred. And as some who have answered aye, may have been changed by the new arguments, the affirmative must be put over again. If then the member entering may, by speaking a few words, occasion a repetition of the question, it would be useless to deny it on his simple call for it.

While the House is telling, no member may speak, or move out of his place; for if any mistake be suspected, it must be told again. *Mem. in Hakew.* 26. 2 *Hats.* 143.

If any difficulty arises in point of order during the division, the Speaker is to decide peremptorily, subject to the future censure of the House if irregular. He sometimes permits old experienced members to assist him with their advice, which they do, sitting in their seats, covered, to avoid the appearance of debate; but this can only be with the Speaker's leave, else the division might last several hours. 2 *Hats.* 143.

The voice of the majority decides. For the lex majoris partis is the law of all councils, elections, &c. where not otherwise expressly provided. *Hakew. 93.* But if the House be equally divided, "semper presumatur pro negante;" that is, the former law is not to be changed but by a majority. *Town. col.* 134.

But in the Senate of the United States, the Vice-President decides, when the House is divided. Constitution United States I. 3.

When from counting the House on a division, it appears that there is not a quorum, the matter continues exactly in the state in which it was before the division, and must be resumed at that point on any future day. 2 *Hats.* 126.

1606, May 1, On a question whether a member having said yea, may afterwards sit and change his opinion? a precedent was remembered by the Speaker, of Mr. Morris, attorney of the wards in 39 *Eliz.* who in like case changed his opinion. *Mem. in Hakew.* 27.

Sec. XLII. TITLE.

AFTER the bill has passed, and not before, the title may be amended, and is to be fixed by a question; and the bill is then sent to the other House.

Sec. XLIII. RECONSIDERATION.

WHEN a question has been once made and carried in the affirmative, or negative, it shall be in order for any member of the majority, to move for the reconsideration thereof. Rule 22.

1798, *January. A bill on its second reading, being amended, and on the question whether it shall be read a third time negatived, was restored by a decision to reconsider that question. Here the votes of negative and reconsideration, like positive and negative quantities in equation, destroy one another, and are as if they were expunged from the journals. Consequently the bill is open for amendment, just so far as it was the moment preceding the question for the third reading. That is to say, all parts of the bill are open for amendment, except those on which votes have been already taken in its present stage. So also it may be recommitted.*

The rule permitting a reconsideration of a question affixing to it no limitation of time or circumstance, it may be asked whether there is no limitation? If, after the vote, the paper on which it is passed has been parted with, there can be no reconsideration: as if a vote has been for the passage of a bill, and the bill has been sent to the other House. But where the paper remains, as on a bill rejected; when, or under what circumstances does it cease to be susceptible of reconsideration? This remains to be settled; unless a sense that the right of reconsideration is a right to waste the time of the House in repeated agitations of the same question, so that it shall never know when a question is done with, should induce them to reform this anomalous proceeding.

In Parliament, a question once carried, cannot be questioned again at the same session; but must stand as the judgment of the House. *Town. col.* 67. *Mem. in Hakew.* 33. And a bill once rejected, another of the same substance cannot be brought in again the same session. *Hakew.* 158. 6 *Grey* 392. But this does not extend to prevent putting the same question in different stages of a bill; because every stage of a bill submits the whole and every part of it to the opinion of the House, as open for amendment, either by insertion or omission, though the same amendment has been accepted or rejected in a former stage. So in reports of committees, e. g. report of an address, the same question is before the House, and open for free discussion. *Town. col.* 26. 2 *Hats.* 98, 100, 101. So orders of the House, or instructions to committees may be discharged. So a bill, begun in one House, sent to the other, and there rejected, may be renewed again in that other, passed and sent back. *Ib.* 92. 3 *Hats.* 161. Or if, instead of being rejected, they read it once and lay it aside, or amend it, and put it off a month, they may order in another to the same effect, with the same or a different title. *Hakew.* 97, 98.

Divers expedients are used to correct the effects of this rule; as by passing an explanatory act, if any thing has been omitted or ill expressed, 3 *Hats.* 278. or an act to enforce, and make more effectual an act, &c. or to rectify mistakes in an act, &c. or a committee on one bill may be instructed to receive a clause to rectify the mistakes of an other. Thus, June 24, 1685, a clause was inserted in a bill for rectifying a mistake committed by a clerk in engrossing a bill of supply. 2 *Hats.* 194, 6. Or the session may be closed for one, two, three or more days, and a new one commenced. But then all matters depending must be finished, or they fall, and are to begin de novo. 2 *Hats.* 94, *to* 98. Or a part of the subject may be taken up by another bill, or taken up in a different way. 6 *Grey* 304, 316.

And in cases of the last magnitude, this rule has not been so strictly and verbally observed as to stop indispensable proceedings altogether. 2 *Hats.* 92, 98. Thus when the address on the preliminaries of peace in 1782 had been lost by a majority of one, on account of the importance of the question, and smallness of the majority, the same question in substance, though with some words not in the first, and which might change the opinion of some members, was brought on again and carried; as the motives for it were thought to outweigh the objection of form. 2 *Hats.* 99, 100.

A second bill may be passed to continue an act of the same session; or to enlarge the time limited for its execution. 2 *Hats.* 95, 98. This is not in contradiction to the first act.

SEC. XLIV. BILLS SENT TO THE OTHER HOUSE.

ALL bills passed in Senate shall, before they are sent to the House of Representatives, be examined by the committees respectively, who brought in such bills, or to whom the same have been last committed in Senate. Rule 23.

A bill from the other House is sometimes ordered to lie on the table. 2 *Hats.* 97.

When bills passed in one House and sent to the other, are grounded on special facts requiring proof, it is usual either by message, or at a conference, to ask the grounds and evidence; and this evidence, whether arising out of papers, or from the examination of witnesses, is immediately communicated. 3 *Hats.* 48.

SEC. XLV. AMENDMENTS BETWEEN THE HOUSES.

WHEN either House, e. g. the House of Commons, sends a bill to the other, the other may pass it with amendments. The regular progression in this case is, that the Commons disagree to the amendment; the Lords insist on it; the Commons insist on their disagreement; the Lords adhere to their amendment; the Commons adhere to their disagreement. The term of insisting, may be repeated as often as they choose, to keep the question open. But the first adherence by either, renders it necessary for the other to recede or adhere also; when the matter is usually suffered to fall. 10 *Grey* 148. Latterly however, there are instances of their having gone to a second adherence. There must be an absolute conclusion of the subject somewhere, or otherwise transactions between the Houses would become endless. 3 *Hats.* 268, 270. The term of insisting, we are told by Sir John Trevor, was then (1679) newly introduced into Parliamentary usage, by the Lords. 7 *Grey* 94. It was certainly a happy innovation, as it multiplies the opportunities of trying modifications which may bring the Houses to a concurrence. Either House however is free to pass over the term of insisting, and to adhere in the first instance. 10 *Grey* 146. But it is not respectful to the other. In the ordinary Parliamentary course, there are two free conferences at least before an adherence. 10 *Grey* 147.

Either House may recede from its amendment and agree to the bill; or recede from their disagreement to the amendment, and agree to the same absolutely, or with an amendment. For here the disagreement and receding destroy one another, and the subject stands as before the disagreement. *Elsynge* 23, 27. 9 *Grey* 476.

But the House cannot recede from, or insist on its own amendment, with an amendment: for the same reason that it cannot send to the other House an amendment to its own act after it has passed the act. They may modify an amendment from the other House by ingrafting an amendment on it, because they have never assented to it; but they cannot amend their own amendment, because they have, on the question, passed it in that form. 9 *Grey* 353. 10 *Grey* 240. In Senate, March 29, 1798. Nor where one House has adhered to their amendment, and the other agrees with an amendment, can the first House depart from the form which they have fixed by an adherence.

In the case of a money bill, the Lords proposed amendments, become by delay, confessedly necessary. The Commons however, refused them, as infringing on their privilege as to money bills; but they offered themselves to add to the bill a proviso to the same effect, which had no coherence with the Lords' amendments; and urged that it was an expedient warranted by precedent, and not unparliamentary, in a case become impracticable and irremediable in any other way. 3 *Hats.* 256, 266, 270, 271. But the Lords refused, and the bill was lost. 1 *Chand.* 288. A like case, 1 *Chand.* 311. So the Commons resolve that it is unparliamentary to strike out at a conference any thing in a bill which hath been agreed and passed by both Houses. 6 *Grey* 274. 1 *Chand.* 312.

A motion to amend an amendment from the other House, takes precedence of a motion to agree or disagree.

A bill originating in one House, is passed by the other with an amendment. The originating House agrees to their amendment with an amendment. The other may agree to their amendment with an amendment; that being only in the second and not the third degree. For as to the amending House, the first amendment with which they passed the bill, is a part of its text; it is the only text they have agreed to. The amendment to that text by the originating House, therefore, is only in the first degree, and the amendment to that again by the amending House is only in the second, to wit, an amendment to an amendment, and so admissible. Just so when, on a bill from the originating House, the other, at its second reading, makes an amendment; on the third reading, this amendment is become the text of the bill, and if an amendment to it be moved, an amendment to that amendment may also be moved, as being only in the second degree.

Sec. XLVI. CONFERENCES.

IT is on the occasion of amendments **by one House disagreed to by the other,** that conferences are usually asked; but they may be asked **4 *Hats.* 4, 223,** in all cases of difference of opinion between the two Houses, on matters depending between them. **4 *Hats.* 4, 5, 7.** The request of a conference, however, must always be by the House which is possessed of the papers. 3 *Hats.* 31. 1 *Grey* 425. **4 *Hats.* 3, 43.**[20]

Conferences may be either simple or free. At a conference simply, written reasons are prepared by the House asking it, and they are read and delivered, without debate, to the managers of the other House at the conference; but are not then to be answered. 3 *Grey* 144.[21] The other House then, if satisfied, vote the reasons satisfactory, or say nothing; if not satisfied, they resolve them not satisfactory, and ask a conference on the subject of the last conference, where they read and deliver in like manner written answers to those reasons. 3 *Grey* 183. They are meant, chiefly, to record the justification of each House to the nation

---

20 Jefferson made the following annotation to Sec. 46, Para. 1 in the Library copy and the Holmes copy: "by one house disagreed to by the other," which was printed in Milligan's 1812 edition. This replaced "between the houses" in Smith's 1801 edition. "4. Hats. 4, 223" is an annotation by Jefferson in the Library copy and the Holmes copy and is printed in Milligan's 1812 edition. "4. Hats. 4, 5, 7" and "4. Hats. 3, 43" are annotations in the Library copy and are printed in Milligan's 1812 edition.

21 In the Library copy, Jefferson adds the annotation "4. Hats. 47, 32." at the end of this sentence in Sec. 46, Para. 2; it is not printed in Milligan's 1812 edition.

at large, and to posterity, and in proof that the miscarriage of a necessary measure is not imputable to them. 3 *Grey* 255. At free conferences, **which are asked after two conferences, 4 *Hats.* 37, 40.**[22] the managers discuss viva voce and freely, and interchange propositions for such modifications as may be made in a Parliamentary way, and may bring the sense of the two Houses together. **The conferees may argue in support of what is done in their House, but not against it, nor assent to any new thing there propounded, till their House be informed and agree to it. 4 *Hats.* 31, 33.**[23] And each party reports in writing to their respective Houses, the substance of what is said on both sides, and it is entered in their journals. 9 *Grey* 220. 3 *Hats.* 280. **4 *Hats.* 48.**[24] This report cannot be amended or altered, as that of a committee may be. *Journ. Sen. May* 24, 1796.

A conference may be asked before the House asking it has come to a resolution of disagreement, insisting or adhering.[25] *3 Hats.* 269, 341.[26] In which case the papers are not left with the other conferees, but are brought back to be the foundation of the vote to be given. And this is the most reasonable and respectful

22 "... which are asked after two conferences, 4. *Hats.* 37, 40." is an annotation by Jefferson in the Library copy and the Holmes copy, which is printed in Milligan's 1812 edition.

23 "The conferees may ... 4. *Hats.* 31, 33" is an annotation by Jefferson in Sec. 46, Para. 2 in the Library copy and the Holmes copy, which is printed in Milligan's 1812 edition.

24 "4 *Hats.* 48" is an annotation by Jefferson in Sec. 46, Para. 2 in the Library copy and is printed in Milligan's 1812 edition.

25 Howell italicizes this sentence, but it is not italicized in Smith's 1801 or Milligan's 1812 editions, there is no annotation by Jefferson on this text, nor does it appear to be peculiar to the Senate.

26 In the Library copy, Jefferson adds the annotation "4. *Hats.* 4" in Sec. 46, Para. 3 in the right margin adjacent to the end of this sentence. This annotation is not printed in Milligan's 1812 edition.

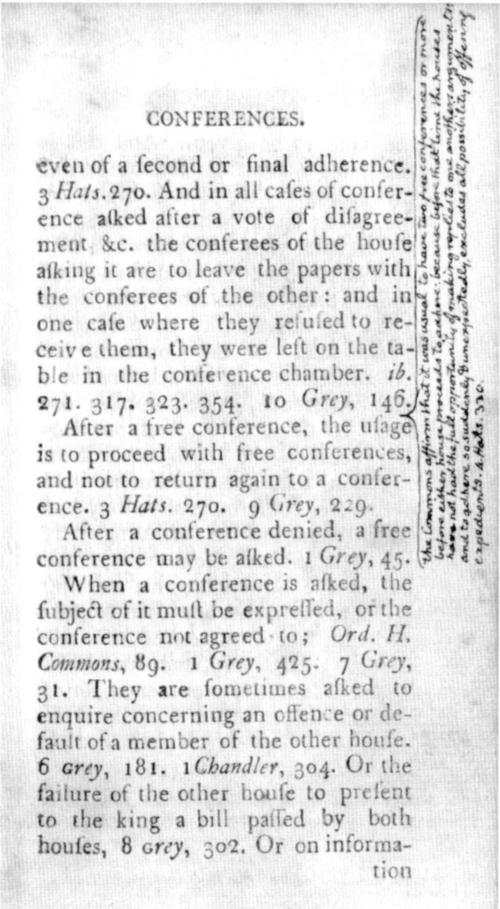

CONFERENCES.

even of a fecond or final adherence. 3 *Hats*. 270. And in all cafes of conference afked after a vote of difagreement, &c. the conferees of the houfe afking it are to leave the papers with the conferees of the other: and in one cafe where they refufed to receive them, they were left on the table in the conference chamber. *ib.* 271. 317. 323. 354. 10 *Grey*, 146.

After a free conference, the ufage is to proceed with free conferences, and not to return again to a conference. 3 *Hats*. 270. 9 *Grey*, 229.

After a conference denied, a free conference may be afked. 1 *Grey*, 45.

When a conference is afked, the fubject of it muft be expreffed, or the conference not agreed to; *Ord. H. Commons*, 89. 1 *Grey*, 425. 7 *Grey*, 31. They are fometimes afked to enquire concerning an offence or default of a member of the other houfe. 6 *Grey*, 181. 1 *Chandler*, 304. Or the failure of the other houfe to prefent to the king a bill paffed by both houfes, 8 *Grey*, 302. Or on information-

tion

the Commons affirm that it was usual to have two free conferences or more before either house proceeds to adhere: because before that time the houses have not had the full opportunity of making replies to one another's arguments, and to adhere so suddenly & unexpectedly excludes all possibility of offering expedients. 4. Hats. 330.

Figure 10. Jefferson's *Manual* (1801) (detail, Section 46), with annotations to the text by Jefferson, presented to Hugh Holmes, 22 December 1803.

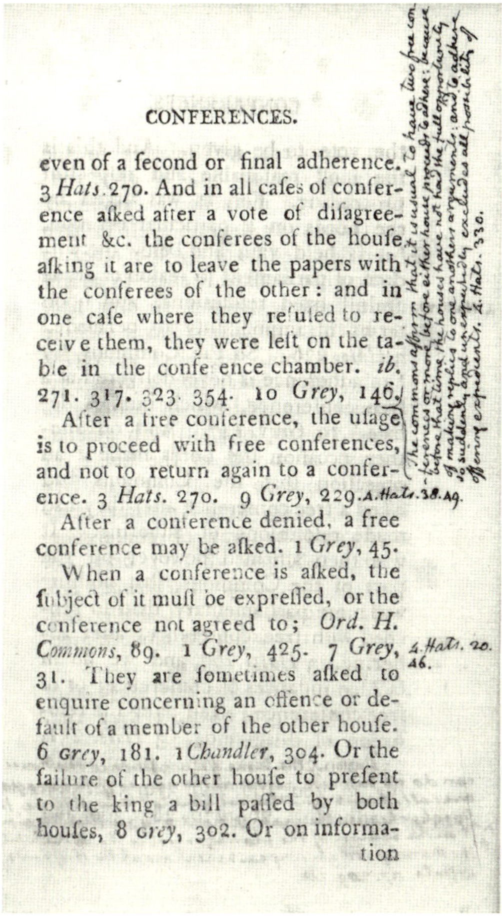

CONFERENCES.

even of a ſecond or final adherence. 3 *Hats*. 270. And in all caſes of conference aſked after a vote of diſagreement &c. the conferees of the houſe aſking it are to leave the papers with the conferees of the other: and in one caſe where they refuſed to receive them, they were left on the table in the conference chamber. *ib.* 271. 317. 323. 354. 10 *Grey*, 146.

[The commons affirm that it is usual to have two free conferences or more before either house proceeds to adhere; because before that time the houses have not had the full opportunity of making replies to one another's arguments; and to adhere so suddenly and unexpectedly excludes all possibility of offering expedients. 4. Hats. 330.]

After a free conference, the uſage is to proceed with free conferences, and not to return again to a conference. 3 *Hats*. 270. 9 *Grey*, 229. 4. Hats. 38. 49.

After a conference denied, a free conference may be aſked. 1 *Grey*, 45.

When a conference is aſked, the ſubject of it muſt be expreſſed, or the conference not agreed to; *Ord. H. Commons*, 89. 1 *Grey*, 425. 7 *Grey*, 31. 4. Hats. 20. 46. They are ſometimes aſked to enquire concerning an offence or default of a member of the other houſe. 6 *Grey*, 181. 1 *Chandler*, 304. Or the failure of the other houſe to preſent to the king a bill paſſed by both houſes, 8 *Grey*, 302. Or on information

FIGURE 11. Jefferson's *Manual* (1801) (detail, Section 46), with annotations to the text by Thomas Jefferson, Library of Congress, volume 4.

proceeding. For, as was urged by the Lords on a particular occasion, "it is held vain and below the wisdom of Parliament to reason or argue against fixed resolutions, and upon terms of impossibility to persuade." 3 *Hats.* 226. So the Commons say "an adherence is never delivered at a free conference, which implies debate." 10 *Grey* 147. And on another occasion, the Lords made it an objection that the Commons had asked a free conference after they had made resolutions of adhering. It was then affirmed, however, on the part of the Commons, that nothing was more Parliamentary than to proceed with free conferences after adhering; 3 *Hats.* 269. and we do in fact see instances of conference, or of free conference, asked after the resolution of disagreeing, 3 *Hats.* 251, 253, 260, 286, 291, 316, 239; of insisting, *ib.* 280, 296, 299, 319, 322, 355;[27] of adhering, 269, 270, 283, 300;[28] and even of a second or final adherence, 3 *Hats.* 270. And in all cases of conference asked after a vote of disagreement, &c. the conferees of the House asking it, are to leave the papers with the conferees of the other: and in one case, where they refused to receive them, they were left on the table in the conference chamber. *Ib.* 271, 317, 323, 354. 10 *Grey* 146.

The Commons affirm that it is usual to have two free conferences or more, before either House proceeds to adhere: because, before that time, the Houses have not had the full opportunity of making replies to one another's arguments; and to adhere so suddenly and unexpectedly, excludes all possibility of offering expedients. 4 *Hats.* 330.[29]

27 In the Library copy, Jefferson adds the annotation "4. *Hats.* 43." in Sec. 46, Para. 3, which is not printed in Milligan's 1812 edition.

28 In the Library copy, Jefferson adds the annotation "4. *Hats.* 39, 41." in Sec. 46, Para. 3, which is not printed in Milligan's 1812 edition.

29 "The Commons affirm... 4 *Hats.* 330" is an annotation added by Jefferson in

After a free conference, the usage is to proceed with free conferences, and not to return again to a conference. 3 *Hats.* 270. 9 *Grey* 229.[30]

After a conference denied, a free conference may be asked. 1 *Grey* 45.

When a conference is asked, the subject of it must be expressed, or the conference not agreed to. *Ord. H. Commons* 89. 1 *Grey* 425. 7 *Grey* 31. **4 *Hats.* 20, 46.**[31] They are sometimes asked to enquire concerning an offence, or default of a member of the other House. 6 *Grey* 181. 1 *Chandler* 304. Or the failure of the other House to present to the king a bill passed by both Houses. 8 *Grey* 302. Or on information received, and relating to the safety of the nation. 10 *Grey* 171. Or, when the methods of Parliament are thought by the one House to have been departed from by the other, a conference is asked to come to a right understanding thereon. 10 *Grey* 148.[32] So when an unparliamentary message has been sent, instead of answering it, they ask a conference. 3 *Grey* 155. Formerly, an address, or articles of impeachment, or a bill with amendments, or a vote of the House, or concurrence in a vote, or a message from the king, were sometimes communicated by way of conference. 6 *Grey* 128, 300, 387. 7 *Grey* 80. 8 *Grey* 210, 255. 1 *Torbuck's Deb.* 278. 10 *Grey* 293. 1 *Chandler* 49, 287. But this is not the modern practice. 8 *Grey* 255.

Sec. 46, Para. 4 in the Library copy and the Holmes copy, which is printed in Milligan's 1812 edition.

30 In the Library copy, Jefferson adds the annotation "4. *Hats.* 38, 49." in Sec. 46, Para. 5, which is not printed in Milligan's 1812 edition.

31 "4. *Hats.* 20, 46" is an annotation added by Jefferson in Sec. 46, Para. 7 in the Library copy, which is printed in Milligan's 1812 edition.

32 In the Library copy, Jefferson adds the annotation "4. *Hats.* 21." in Sec. 46, Para. 7, which is not printed in Milligan's 1812 edition.

A conference has been asked after the first reading of a bill. 1 *Grey* 194. This is a singular instance.

During the time of a conference the House can do no business. As soon as the names of the managers are called over, and they are gone to the conference, the Speaker leaves the chair, without any question, and resumes it on the return of the managers. It is the same while the managers of an impeachment are at the House of Lords. 4 *Hats.* 47, 209, 288.[33]

Sec. XLVII. MESSAGES.

MESSAGES between the Houses are to be sent only while both Houses are sitting. 3 *Hats.* 15. They are received during a debate, without adjourning the debate. *3 Hats. 22.*

In Senate the messengers are introduced in any state of business, except, 1. *While a question is putting.* 2. *While the Yeas and Nays are calling.* 3. *While the ballots are calling. The first case is short: the second and third are cases where any interruption might occasion errors difficult to be corrected. So arranged June* 15, 1798.

In the House of Representatives, as in Parliament, if the House be in committee when a messenger attends, the Speaker takes the chair to receive the message, and then quits it to return into committee, without any question or interruption. 4 *Grey* 226.

Messengers are not saluted by the members, but by the Speaker for the House. 2 *Grey* 253, 274.

---

33 "During the time of... 4 *Hats.* 47, 209, 288." is an annotation by Jefferson in Sec. 46, Para. 9 in the Library copy and the Holmes copy, which is printed in Milligan's 1812 edition.

If messengers commit an error in delivering their message, they may be admitted, or called in, to correct their message. 4 *Grey* 41.[34] Accordingly, March 13, 1800, the Senate having made two amendments to a bill from the House of Representatives, their secretary, by mistake, delivered one only; which being inadmissible by itself, that House disagreed, and notified the Senate of their disagreement. This produced a discovery of the mistake. The secretary was sent to the other House to correct his mistake, the correction was received, and the two amendments acted on de novo.

As soon as the messenger who has brought bills from the other House, has retired, the Speaker holds the bill in his hand, and acquaints the House "that the other House have, by their messenger, sent certain bills," and then reads their titles, and delivers them to the clerk to be safely kept, till they shall be called for to be read. *Hak.* 178.

It is not the usage for one House to inform the other by what numbers a bill has passed. 10 *Grey* 150.[35] Yet they have sometimes recommended a bill, as of great importance to the consideration of the House to which it is sent. 3 *Hats.* 25. Nor when they have rejected a bill from the other House, do they give notice of it; but it passes sub silentio, to prevent unbecoming altercations. 1 *Blackst.* 183.

But in Congress, the rejection is notified by message to the House in which the bill originated.

A question is never asked by the one House of the other by way

34 In the Library copy, Jefferson adds the annotation "4. *Hats.* 16." in Sec. 47, Para. 5, which is not printed in Milligan's 1812 edition.

35 In the Library copy, Jefferson adds the annotation "4. *Hats.* 324." in Sec. 47, Para. 7, which is not printed in Milligan's 1812 edition.

of message, but only at a conference: for this is an interrogatory, not a message. 3 *Grey* 151, 181.

When a bill is sent by one House to the other, and is neglected, they may send a message to remind them of it. 3 *Hats.* 25. 5 *Grey* 154. But if it be mere inattention, it is better to have it done informally, by communications between the Speakers, or members of the two Houses.

Where the subject of a message is of a nature that it can properly be communicated to both Houses of Parliament, it is expected that this communication should be made to both on the same day. But where a message was accompanied with an original declaration, signed by the party to which the message referred, its being sent to one House was not noticed by the other, because the declaration, being original, could not possibly be sent to both Houses at the same time. 2 *Hats.* 260, 261, 262.

The king having sent original letters to the Commons, afterwards desires they may be returned, that he may communicate them to the Lords. 1 *Chandler* 303.

Sec. XLVIII. ASSENT.

THE House which has received a bill and passed it, may present it for the king's assent, and ought to do it, though they have not by message notified to the other, their passage of it. Yet the notifying by message is a form which ought to be observed between the two Houses from motives of respect, and good understanding. 2 *Hats.* 242. Were the bill to be withheld from being presented to the king, it would be an infringement of the rules of Parliament. *Ib.*

When a bill has passed both Houses of Congress, the House last acting on it, notifies its passage to the other, and delivers the bill to the joint committee of enrollment, who see that it is truly enrolled in parchment. When the bill is enrolled, it is not to be written in paragraphs, but solidly and all of a piece, that the blanks between the paragraphs may not give room for forgery. 9 *Grey* 143. *It is then put into the hands of the clerk of the House of Representatives to have it signed by the Speaker. The clerk then brings it by way of message to the Senate to be signed by their President. The secretary of the Senate returns it to the committee of enrollment, who present it to the President of the United States. If he approves, he signs and deposits it among the rolls in the office of the secretary of state, and notifies by message the House in which it originated, that he has approved and signed it; of which that House informs the other by message. If the President disapproves, he is to return it, with his objections, to that House in which it shall have originated; who are to enter the objections at large on their journal, and proceed to reconsider it. If after such reconsideration, two thirds of that House shall agree to pass the bill, it shall be sent, together with the President's objections, to the other House, by which it shall likewise be reconsidered; and if approved by two thirds of that House, it shall become a law. If any bill shall not be returned by the President within ten days (Sunday excepted) after it shall have been presented to him, the same shall be a law, in like manner as if he had signed it, unless the Congress, by their adjournment, prevent its return; in which case it shall not be a law.* Constitution United States, I. 7.

Every order, resolution, or vote, to which the concurrence of the Senate and House of Representatives may be necessary, (except on a question of adjournment,) shall be presented to the President of the United States, and before the same shall take effect, shall be approved by him, or being disapproved by him, shall be repassed by two thirds of the Senate and House of Representatives, according to the rules and limitations prescribed in the case of a bill. Constitution United States, I. 7.

SEC. XLIX. JOURNALS.

EACH House shall keep a journal of its proceedings, and from time to time publish the same, excepting such parts as may, in their judgment, require secrecy. Constitution I. 5.

Every vote of Senate shall be entered on the journals, and a brief statement of the contents of each petition, memorial or paper, presented to the Senate, be also inserted on the journals. Rule 24.[36]

The proceedings of the Senate, when not acting as in a committee of the House, shall be entered on the journals, as concisely as possible, care being taken to detail a true account of the proceedings. Rule 26.

The titles of bills, and such parts thereof only as shall be affected by proposed amendments, shall be inserted on the journals. Rule 27.

If a question is interrupted by a vote to adjourn, or to proceed to the orders of the day, the original question is never printed in the journal, it never having been a vote, nor introductory to any vote: but when suppressed by the previous question, the

36 At this place in the *Manual*, Howell inserts a new paragraph for Rule 25, although the paragraph does not appear in Smith's 1801 or Milligan's 1812 editions: "*The proceedings of Senate, when they shall act in their Executive capacity shall be kept in separate & distinct books.* Rule 25" (Howell, *Parliamentary Writings*, 416). Howell offers compelling justification for this insertion based on extensive detail drawn from Jefferson's notes; see Howell, *Parliamentary Writings*, 432.

first question must be stated, in order to introduce and make intelligible the second. 2 *Hats.* 83.

So also when a question is postponed, adjourned, or laid on the table, the original question, though not yet a vote, must be expressed in the journals; because it makes part of the vote of postponement, adjourning, or laying it on the table.

Where amendments are made to a question, those amendments are not printed in the journals separated from the question; but only the question as finally agreed to by the House. The rule of entering in the journals only what the House has agreed to, is founded in great prudence and good sense; as there may be many questions proposed which it may be improper to publish to the world, in the form in which they are made. 2 *Hats.* 85.

In both Houses of Congress all questions whereon the Yeas and Nays are desired by one fifth of the members present, whether decided affirmatively or negatively, must be entered in the journals. Constitution I. 5.

The first order for printing the votes of the House of Commons, was October 30, 1685. 1 *Chandler* 387.

Some judges have been of opinion, that the journals of the House of Commons are no records, but only remembrances. But this is not law. *Hob.* 110, 111. *Lex. Parl.* 114, 115. *Journ. H. C. Mar.* 17, 1592. *Hale Parl.* 105. For the Lords in their House have power of judicature, the Commons in their House have power of judicature, and both Houses together have power of judicature; and the book of the clerk of the House of Commons is a record, as is affirmed by act of Parliament; 6 *H.* 8. *c.* 16. 4 *Inst.* 23, 24. and every member of the House of Commons hath a judicial place. 4 *Inst.* 15. As records, they are open to every person, and a printed vote of either House is sufficient ground for the other to notice it. Either may appoint a committee to inspect the journals of the other, and report what has been done by the other in any particular case. 2 *Hats.* 261. 3 *Hats.* 27, 30. Every member has a right to see the journals, and to take and publish votes from them. Being a record, every one may see and publish them. 6 *Grey* 118, 119.

On information of a misentry or omission of an entry in the journal, a committee may be appointed to examine and rectify it, and report it to the House. 2 *Hats.* 194, 5.

Sec. L. ADJOURNMENT.

THE two Houses of Parliament have the sole, separate, and independent power of adjourning each their respective Houses. The king has no authority to adjourn them; he can only signify his desire, and it is in the wisdom and prudence of either House to comply with his requisition, or not, as they see fitting. 2 *Hats.* 232. 1 *Blackstone* 186. 5 *Grey* 122.

By the Constitution of the United States, a smaller number than a majority may adjourn from day to day. I. 5. *But "neither House, during the session of Congress, shall, without the consent of the other, adjourn for more than three days, nor to any other place than that in which the two Houses shall be sitting."* I. 5. *And in case of disagreement between them with respect to the time of adjournment, the President may adjourn them to such time as he shall think proper.* Constitution II. 3.

A motion to adjourn simply, cannot be amended as by adding "to a particular day." But must be put simply "that this House do now adjourn?" and if carried in the affirmative, it is adjourned to the next sitting day, unless it has come to a previous resolution "that at its rising it will adjourn to a particular day," and then the House is adjourned to that day. 2 *Hats.* 82.

Where it is convenient that the business of the House be suspended for a short time, as for a conference presently to be held, &c. it adjourns during pleasure. 2 *Hats.* 305. Or for a quarter of an hour. 5 *Grey* 331.

If a question be put for adjournment, it is no adjournment till the Speaker pronounces it. 5 *Grey* 137. And from courtesy and respect, no member leaves his place till the Speaker has passed on.

Sec. LI. A SESSION.

PARLIAMENT have three modes of separation, to wit, by adjournment, by prorogation, or dissolution by the king, or by the efflux of the term for which they were elected. Prorogation or dissolution constitutes there what is called a session, provided some act has passed. In this case, all matters depending before them are discontinued, and at their next meeting are to be taken up de novo, if taken up at all. 1 *Blackst.* 186. Adjournment, which is by themselves, is no more than a continuance of the session from one day to another, or for a fortnight, a month, &c. ad libitum. All matters depending remain in statu quo, and when they meet again, be the term ever so distant, are resumed without any fresh commencement, at the point at which they were left. 1 *Lev.* 165. *Lex. Parl. c.* 2. 1 *Ro. Rep.* 29. 4 *Inst.* 7, 27, 28. *Hutt.* 61. 1 *Mod.* 252. *Ruffh. Jac. L.*

Dict. Parliament. 1 *Blackst.* 186. Their whole session is considered in law but as one day, and has relation to the first day thereof. *Bro. Abr. Parliament* 86.

Committees may be appointed to sit during a recess by adjournment, but not by prorogation. 5 *Grey* 374. 9 *Grey* 350. 1 *Chandler* 50. Neither House can continue any portion of itself in any Parliamentary function beyond the end of the session, without the consent of the other two branches. When done, it is by a bill constituting them commissioners for the particular purpose.

Congress separate in two ways only, to wit, by adjournment, or dissolution by the efflux of their time. What then constitutes a session with them? A dissolution certainly closes one session, and the meeting of the new Congress begins another. The constitution authorises the President "on extraordinary occasions, to convene both Houses or either of them." I. 3. *If convened by the President's proclamation, this must begin a new session, and of course determine the preceding one to have been a session. So if it meets under the clause of the constitution which says, "the Congress shall assemble at least once in every year, and such meeting shall be on the first Monday in December, unless they shall by law appoint a different day,"* I. 4. *this must begin a new session. For even if the last adjournment was to this day, the act of adjournment is merged in the higher authority of the constitution, and the meeting will be under that, and not under their adjournment. So far we have fixed land marks for determining sessions. In other cases, it is declared by the joint vote authorising the President of the Senate and the Speaker to close the session on a fixed day, which is usually in the following form, "Resolved by the Senate and House of Representatives, that the President of the Senate*

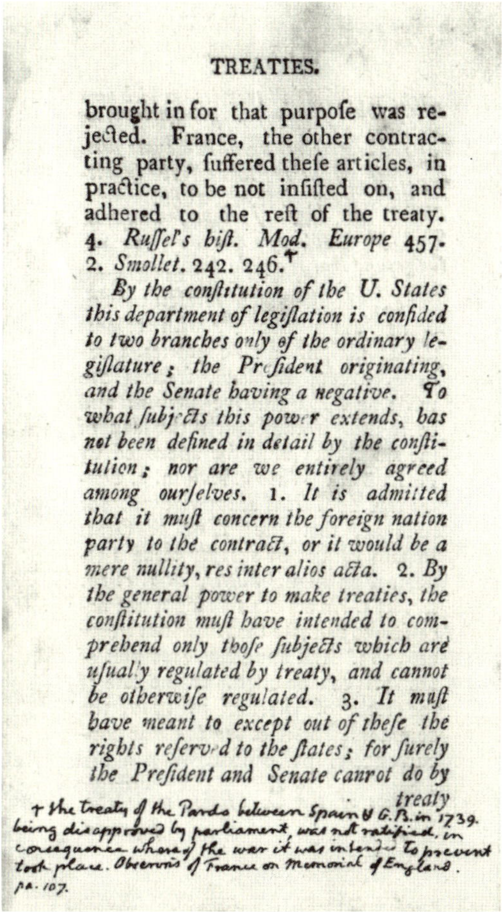
TREATIES.

brought in for that purpoſe was rejected. France, the other contracting party, ſuffered theſe articles, in practice, to be not inſiſted on, and adhered to the reſt of the treaty. 4. *Ruſſel's hiſt. Mod. Europe* 457. 2. *Smollet*. 242. 246.†

By the conſtitution of the U. States this department of legiſlation is confided to two branches only of the ordinary legiſlature; the Preſident originating, and the Senate having a negative. To what ſubjects this power extends, has not been defined in detail by the conſtitution; nor are we entirely agreed among ourſelves. 1. *It is admitted that it muſt concern the foreign nation party to the contract, or it would be a mere nullity, res inter alios acta.* 2. *By the general power to make treaties, the conſtitution muſt have intended to comprehend only thoſe ſubjects which are uſually regulated by treaty, and cannot be otherwiſe regulated.* 3. *It muſt have meant to except out of theſe the rights reſerved to the ſtates; for ſurely the Preſident and Senate cannot do by*

treaty

† the treaty of the Pardo between Spain & G.B. in 1739. being disapproved by parliament, was not ratified, in consequence whereof the war it was intended to prevent took place. Observns of France on Memorial of England. pa. 107.

FIGURE 12. Jefferson's *Manual* (1801) (detail, Section 53), with annotations to the text by Jefferson, presented to Francis Taliaferro Brooke, 20 December 1802. The text of this annotation appears nowhere else and is unique to the Brooke copy alone.

and the Speaker of the House of Representatives, be authorised to close the present session, by adjourning their respective Houses on the —— day of ——."

When it was said above, that all matters depending before Parliament were discontinued by the determination of the session, it was not meant for judiciary cases, depending before the House of Lords, such as impeachments, appeals, and writs of error. These stand continued of course, to the next session. *Raym.* 120, 381, *Ruffh. Jac. L. D. Parliament.*

Impeachments stand in like manner continued before the Senate of the United States.

Sec. LII. TREATIES.

THE President of the United States has power, by and with the advice and consent of the Senate, to make treaties, provided two thirds of the Senators present concur. Constitution United States II. 2.

Resolved that all confidential communications, made by the President of the United States to the Senate, shall be, by the members thereof, kept inviolably secret; and that all treaties, which may hereafter be laid before the Senate shall also be kept secret until the Senate shall, by their resolution, take off the injunction of secrecy. December 22, 1800.

Treaties are legislative acts. A treaty is a law of the land. It differs from other laws only as it must have the consent of a foreign nation, being but a contract with respect to that nation. In all countries, I believe, except England, treaties are made by the legislative power: and there also, if they touch the laws of the land, they must be approved by Parliament. *Ware v. Hylton. 3 Dallas Rep.* 273. It is acknowledged, for instance, that the king of Great Britain cannot by a treaty make a citizen of an alien. *Vattel. B.* 1. *c.* 19. *sec.* 214. An act of Parliament was necessary to validate the American treaty of 1783. And abundant examples of such acts can be cited. In the case of the treaty of Utretcht in 1712, the commercial articles required the concurrence of Parliament.[37] But a bill brought in for that purpose was rejected. France, the other contracting party, suffered these articles, in practice, to be not insisted on, and adhered to the rest of the treaty. 4 *Russel's Hist. Mod. Europe* 457. 2 *Smollet* 242, 246.[38]

By the Constitution of the United States, this department of legislation is confided to two branches only of the ordinary legislature; the President originating, and the Senate having a negative. To what subjects this power extends, has not been defined in detail by the constitution; nor are we entirely agreed among ourselves. 1. *It is admitted that it must concern the foreign nation party to the contract, or it would be a mere nullity, res inter alios acta.* 2. *By the general power to make treaties, the constitution must have intended to comprehend only those subjects which are usually regulated by treaty, and cannot be otherwise regulated.* 3. *It must have meant to except out of these the rights reserved to the states; for surely the President and Senate cannot do by treaty what the whole government is interdicted from doing in any way.*

37 In both Smith's 1801 and Milligan's 1812 editions, the name of the city Utrecht is spelled "Utretcht."

38 In the Brooke copy, Jefferson adds the following annotation: "†The treaty of the Pardo between Spain & G.B. in 1739. being disapproved by parliament, was not ratified. In consequence whereof the war it was intended to prevent took place. Observns. of France on Memorial of England. pa. 107." This text is exclusive to the Brooke copy and does not appear in Milligan's 1812 edition, the Library copy, or the Holmes copy. See Figure 12.

4. *And also to except those subjects of legislation in which it gave a participation to the House of Representatives. This last exception is denied by some, on the ground that it would leave very little matter for the treaty power to work on. The less the better, say others. The constitution thought it wise to restrain the Executive and Senate from entangling and embroiling our affairs with those of Europe. Besides, as the negotiations are carried on by the Executive alone, the subjecting to the ratification of the Representatives such articles as are within their participation is no more inconvenient than to the Senate. But the ground of this exception is denied as unfounded. For examine, e. g. the treaty of commerce with France, and it will be found that out of thirty one articles, there are not more than small portions of two or three of them which would not still remain as subjects of treaties, untouched by these exceptions.*

Treaties being declared, equally with the laws of the United States, to be the supreme law of the land, it is understood that an act of the legislature alone can declare them infringed and rescinded. This was accordingly the process adopted in the case of France in 1798.

It has been the usage for the Executive, when it communicates a treaty to the Senate for their ratification, to communicate also the correspondence of the negotiators. This having been omitted in the case of the Prussian treaty, was asked by a vote of the House of February 12, 1800, *and was obtained. And in December* 1800, *the convention of that year between the United States and France, with the report of the negotiations by the envoys, but not their instructions, being laid before the Senate, the instructions were asked for and communicated by the President.*

The mode of voting on questions of ratifications is by nominal call.

Resolved, as a standing rule, that whenever a treaty shall be laid before the Senate for ratification, it shall be read a first time for information only; when no motion to reject, ratify or modify the whole or any part shall be received.

That its second reading shall be for consideration; and on a subsequent day, when it shall be taken up as in a committee of the whole, and every one shall be free to move a question on any particular article in this form, "Will the Senate advise and consent to the ratification of this article?" or to propose amendments thereto, either by inserting or by leaving out words, in which last case the question shall be, "Shall the words stand part of the article?" And in every of the said cases, the concurrence of two thirds of the Senators present shall be requisite to decide affirmatively. And when through the whole, the proceedings shall be stated to the House, and questions be again severally put thereon for confirmation, or new ones proposed, requiring in like manner a concurrence of two thirds for whatever is retained or inserted.

That the votes so confirmed shall, by the House, or a committee thereof, be reduced into the form of a ratification, with or without modifications, as may have been decided, and shall be proposed on a subsequent day, when every one shall again be free to move amendments, either by inserting or leaving out words; in which last case the question shall be, "Shall the words stand part of the resolution?" And in both cases the concurrence of two thirds shall be requisite to carry the affirmative; as well as on the final question to advise and consent to the ratification in the form agreed to. Rule of January 6, 1801.

Resolved, that when any question may have been decided by the Senate, in which two thirds of the members present are necessary to carry the affirmative, any member who voted on that side which prevailed in the question, may be at liberty to move for a reconsideration: and a motion for reconsideration shall be decided by a majority of votes. Rule of February 3, 1801.[39]

SEC. LIII. IMPEACHMENT.

THE House of Representatives shall have the sole power of impeachment. Constitution United States, I. 3.

The Senate shall have the sole power to try all impeachments. When sitting for that purpose, they shall be on oath or affirmation. When the President of the United States is tried, the chief justice shall preside: and no person shall be convicted without the concurrence of two thirds of the members present. Judgment in cases of impeachment shall not extend further than to removal from office, and disqualification to hold and enjoy any office of honor, trust, or profit under the United States. But the party convicted shall nevertheless be liable and subject to indictment, trial, judgment and punishment, according to law. Constitution, I. 3.

The President, Vice-President, and all civil officers of the United States, shall be removed from office on impeachment for, and conviction of treason, bribery, or other high crimes and misdemeanors. Constitution, II. 4.

The trial of crimes, except in cases of impeachment, shall be by jury. Constitution, III. 2.

These are the provisions of the Constitution of the United

39 The rules cited as "Rule of January 6, 1801" and "Rule of February 3, 1801" were printed in Smith's 1801 edition; therefore, it seems Jefferson must have provided these additions after submitting the manuscript to Smith in December 1800.

States on the subject of impeachments. The following is a sketch of some of the principles and practices of England on the same subject.

Jurisdiction. The Lords cannot impeach any to themselves, nor join in the accusation, because they are the judges. *Seld. Judic. in Parl.* 12, 63. **(A work of doubtful authority.) 4 *Hats.* 153, 186.**[40] Nor can they proceed against a Commoner but on complaint of the Commons. *Ib.* 84. The Lords may not, by the law, try a Commoner for a capital offence, on the information of the king, or a private person; because the accused is entitled to a trial by his peers generally; but on accusation by the House of Commons, they may proceed against the delinquent of whatsoever degree, and whatsoever be the nature of the offence; for there they do not assume to themselves trial at common law. The Commons are then instead of a jury, and the judgment is given on their demand, which is instead of a verdict. So the Lords do only judge, but not try the delinquent. *Ib.* 6, 7. But Wooddeson denies that a Commoner can now be charged capitally before the Lords, even by the Commons; and cites Fitzharris's case, 1681, impeached of high treason, where the Lords remitted the prosecution to the inferior court. 8 *Grey's Deb.* 325 . . . . 7. 2 *Wooddeson* 601, 576. 3 *Seld.* 1610, 1619, 1641. 4 *Blacks.* 257. 3 *Seld.* 1604, 1618, 9, 1656. **4 *Hats.* 200. *et passim contra.***[41]

Accusation. The Commons, as the grand inquest of the nation, become suitors for penal justice. *2 Wood.* 597. 6 *Grey* 356. The

40 "A work of . . . 186." is an annotation added by Jefferson in Sec. 53, Para. 6 in the Library copy, which is printed in Milligan's 1812 edition.

41 "4 *Hats* . . . contra." is an annotation added by Jefferson in Sec. 53, Para. 6 in the Library copy, which is printed in Milligan's 1812 edition.

general course is, to pass a resolution containing a criminal charge against the supposed delinquent, and then to direct some member to impeach him by oral accusation at the bar of the House of Lords, in the name of the Commons. The person signifies that the articles will be exhibited, and desires that the delinquent may be sequestered from his seat, or be committed, or that the peers will take order for his appearance. *Sachev. Trial.* 325. 2 *Wood.* 602, 605. *Lords' Journ.* 3 *June*, 1701. 1 *Wms.* 616. 6 *Grey* 324.

Process. If the party do not appear, proclamations are to be issued, giving him a day to appear. On their return they are strictly examined. If any error be found in them, a new proclamation issues, giving a short day. If he appear not, his goods may be arrested, and they may proceed. *Seld. Jud.* 98, 99.

Articles. The accusation (articles) of the Commons is substituted in place of an indictment. Thus, by the usage of Parliament, in impeachment for writing or speaking, the particular words need not be specified. *Sach. Tr.* 325. 2 *Wood.* 602, 605. *Lords' Journ.* 3 *June,* 1701. 1 *Wms.* 616.[42]

Appearance. If he appears, and the case be capital, he answers in custody; though not if the accusation be general. He is not to be committed but on special accusations. If it be for a misdemeanor only, he answers a Lord in his place, a Commoner at the bar, and not in custody, unless, on the answer, the Lords find cause to commit him, till he finds sureties to attend, and lest he should fly. *Seld. Jud.* 98, 99. **4 *Hats.* 176, 185.**[43] A copy of the articles is given him, and a day fixed for his answer. *T. Ray.*

42 In the Library copy, Jefferson adds the annotation "4. *Hats.* 283." in Sec. 53, Para. 9, which is not printed in Milligan's 1812 edition.

43 "4 *Hats.* 176, 185" is an annotation added by Jefferson in Sec. 53, Para. 10 in the Library copy, which is printed in Milligan's 1812 edition.

1 *Rushw.* 268. *Fost.* 232. 1 *Clar. Hist. of the Reb.* 379. On a misdemeanor, his appearance may be in person, or he may answer in writing, or by attorney. *Seld. Jud.* 100. The general rule on an accusation for a misdemeanor is, that in such a state of liberty or restraint as the party is when the Commons complain of him, in such he is to answer. *Ib.* 101. If previously committed by the Commons, he answers as a prisoner. But this may be called in some sort judicium parium suorum. *Ib.* In misdemeanors, the party has a right to counsel by the common law; but not in capital cases. *Seld. Jud.* 102 .... 5.

Answer. The answer need not observe great strictness of form. He may plead guilty as to part, and defend as to the residue; or, saving all exceptions, deny the whole, or give a particular answer to each article separately. 1 *Rush.* 274. 2 *Rush.* 1374. 12 *Parl. Hist.* 442. 3 *Lord's Journ.* 13. *Nov.* 1643. 2 *Wood.* 607. But he cannot plead a pardon in bar to the impeachment. 2 *Wood.* 615. 2 *St. Tr.* 735.

Replication, Rejoinder, &c. There may be a replication, rejoinder, &c. *Seld. Jud.* 114. 8 *Grey's Deb.* 233. *Sachev. Tr.* 15. *Journ. H. of Commons, 6 March,* 1640 .... 1.

Witnesses. The practice is to swear the witnesses in open House, and then examine them there: or a committee may be named, who shall examine them in committee, either on interrogatories agreed on in the House, or such as the committee in their discretion shall demand. *Seld. Jud.* 120, 123.

Jury. In the case of Alice Pierce, 1 *R.* 2. a jury was impanelled for her trial before a committee. *Seld. Jud.* 123. But this was on a complaint, not on impeachment by the Commons. *Seld. Jud.* 163. It must also have been for a misdemeanor only, as the Lords spiritual sat in the case, which they do on misdemeanors, but not in capital cases. *Ib.* 148. The judgment was a forfeiture of all her lands and goods. *Ib.* 188. This, Selden says, is the only jury he finds recorded in Parliament for misdemeanors: but he makes no doubt, if the delinquent doth put himself on the trial of his country, a jury ought to be impanelled, and he adds, that it is not so on impeachment by the Commons; for they are in loco proprio, and there no jury ought to be impanelled. *Ib.* 124. The Ld. Berkeley, 6 *E.* 3. was arraigned for the murder of, *E.* 2.[44] on an information on the part of the king, and not on impeachment of the Commons; for then they had been patria sua. He waived his peerage, and was tried by a jury of Gloucestershire and Warwickshire. *Ib.* 125. **But 4 *Hats.* 73, says he was a Commoner, and that there was no waiver of privilege.**[45] In 1 *H.* 7. the Commons protest that they are not to be considered as parties to any judgment given, or hereafter to be given in Parliament. *Ib.* 133. They have been generally, and more justly, considered, as is before stated, as the grand jury. For the conceit of Selden is certainly not accurate, that they are the patria sua of the accused, and that the Lords do only judge, but not try. It is undeniable that they do try. For they examine witnesses as to the facts, and acquit or condemn, according to their own belief of them. And Lord Hale says, "the peers are judges of law as well as of fact." 2 *Hale P. C.* 275. Consequently of fact as well as of law.

---

44 Howell rightly corrects this to "murder of E. 2." although in both Smith's 1801 and Milligan's 1812 editions, it is printed as "L. 2." See Howell, *Parliamentary Writings*, 432–33.

45 "But 4 *Hats*...privilege." is an annotation added by Jefferson in Sec. 53, Para. 14 in the Library copy, which is printed in Milligan's 1812 edition.

Presence of Commons. The Commons are to be present at the examination of witnesses. *Seld. Jud.* 124. Indeed they are to attend throughout, either as a committee of the whole House, or otherwise, at discretion, appoint managers to conduct the proofs. *Rush. Tr. of Straff.* 37. *Com. Journ.* 4 *Feb.* 1709 .... 10. 2 *Wood.* 614. And judgment is not to be given till they demand it. *Seld. Jud.* 124. But they are not to be present on impeachment when the Lords consider of the answer or proofs, and determine of their judgment. Their presence however is necessary at the answer and judgment in cases capital, *ib.* 158, 159, as well as not capital. 162. The Lords debate the judgment among themselves. Then the vote is first taken on the question of guilty or not guilty: and if they convict, the question, or particular sentence, is out of that which seemeth to be most generally agreed on. *Seld. Jud.* 167. 2 *Wood.* 612.

Judgment. Judgments in Parliament for death have been strictly guided per legem terræ, which they cannot alter: and not at all according to their discretion. They can neither omit any part of the legal judgment, nor add to it. Their sentence must be secundum, non ultra legem. *Seld. Jud.* 168, 171. This trial, though it varies in external ceremony, yet differs not in essentials from criminal prosecutions before inferior courts. The same rules of evidence, the same legal notions of crimes and punishments prevail. For impeachments are not framed to alter the law, but to carry it into more effectual execution against two powerful delinquents. The judgment therefore is to be such as is warranted by legal principles or precedents. 6 *Sta. Tr.* 14. 2 *Wood.* 611. The Chancellor gives judgments in misdemeanors; the Lord High Steward formerly in cases of life and death. *Seld. Jud.* 180.[46] But now the Steward is deemed not necessary. *Fost.* 144. 2 *Wood.* 613.[47] In misdemeanors, the greatest corporal punishment hath been imprisonment. *Seld. Jud.* 184. The king's assent is necessary in capital judgments, (but 2 *Wood.* 614, contra) but not in misdemeanors. *Seld. Jud.* 136.

Continuance. An impeachment is not discontinued by the dissolution of Parliament; but may be resumed by the new Parliament. *T. Ray.* 383. 4 *Com. Journ.* 23 *Dec.* 1790. *Lords' Journ. May* 16, 1791. 2 *Wood.* 618.[48]

THE END.

46 In the Library copy, Jefferson adds the annotation "4. *Hats.* 186." in Sec. 53, Para. 16, which is not printed in Milligan's 1812 edition.

47 In the Library copy, Jefferson adds the annotation "4. *Hats.* 191." in Sec. 53, Para. 16, which is not printed in Milligan's 1812 edition.

48 In the Library copy, Jefferson adds the annotation "4. *Hats.* 181. 185. 253." in Sec. 53, Para. 17, which is not printed in Milligan's 1812 edition.

INDEX.[49]

49 This index appeared in both Smith's 1801 and Milligan's 1812 editions of the *Manual.*

Illustration Credits

FRONTISPIECE.

Washington and Lee University; University Collections of Art and History; Bequest of Dr. William Newton Mercer, 1875; photograph courtesy of Museums at Washington and Lee University.

FIGURE 1.

Washington and Lee University, Special Collections; photograph courtesy of Washington and Lee University.

FIGURE 2.

Photograph by Brian Alexander, with courtesy of Independence National Historical Park, August 2020.

FIGURE 3.

Copy 4, Library of Congress, Rare Book and Special Collections Division, Washington, D.C.; photograph courtesy of Library of Congress.

FIGURES 4A AND 4B.

Copy 4, Library of Congress, Rare Book and Special Collections Division, Washington, D.C.; photograph courtesy of Library of Congress.

FIGURE 5.

The Papers of Thomas Jefferson, Princeton University; photostatic image courtesy of Princeton University.

FIGURE 6.

Washington and Lee University, Special Collections; photograph courtesy of Washington and Lee University.

FIGURE 7.

Washington and Lee University, Special Collections; photograph by Byron Faidley.

FIGURE 8.

Washington and Lee University, Special Collections; photograph courtesy of Washington and Lee University.

FIGURE 9.

Copy 4, Library of Congress, Rare Book and Special Collections Division, Washington, D.C.; photograph courtesy of Library of Congress.

FIGURE 10.

Washington and Lee University, Special Collections; photograph courtesy of Washington and Lee University.

FIGURE 11.

Copy 4, Library of Congress, Rare Book and Special Collections Division, Washington, D.C.; photograph courtesy of Library of Congress.

FIGURE 12.

The Papers of Thomas Jefferson, Princeton University; photostatic image courtesy of Princeton University.

ABOUT THE AUTHOR

Brian Alexander, Ph.D., is Associate Professor of Politics at Washington and Lee University. His teaching and research focus on American government and US foreign policy, with publications that include *A Social Theory of Congress: Legislative Norms in the Twenty-First Century* (Rowman & Littlefield 2021) and *The Folkways of Congress*, editor (Brookings Institution Press 2026). He is director of the W&L Washington Term, an experiential learning program for college students in Washington, DC. Brian also served as American Political Science Association Congressional Fellow (2015–2016) in the office of U.S. Senator Jack Reed (D-RI). In 2021, he held a fellowship at the International Center for Jefferson Studies at Monticello, where he conducted research on Thomas Jefferson and parliamentary law. Prior to joining W&L, Brian worked as a management consultant serving federal agency clients and in numerous non-profits focused on foreign and domestic policy. He holds a Ph.D. in Political Science from George Mason University and an undergraduate degree from Miami University. He lives in Lexington, Virginia, with his wife and two daughters.